RELIGION IN LIFE

A Religious Education Course
for Secondary Schools

1. Religious Buildings and Festivals

by
John R. Bailey

SCHOFIELD & SIMS LTD., HUDDERSFIELD

0 7217 3033 7

First printed 1984

Typesetting by PFB Art & Type Ltd., Leeds
Printed in England by Chorley & Pickersgill Ltd., Leeds

Introduction

This series of books is intended to provide a foundation for a five-year course in Religious Education in the Secondary school. Each book contains fifty units of work, each of which forms the basis of one lesson or period.

The course follows a thematic approach to the study of religion, as recommended by many recent Agreed Syllabuses for Religious Education. The approach is open-ended and questioning, recognising that in a multi-faith society, the aim of Religious Education must be:

"to enable pupils to reflect upon their experience and upon mankind's quest for and expression of meaning in life; and to acquire an understanding of religious beliefs and practices, and the importance and influence of these in the lives of believers." (Lincolnshire Agreed Syllabus.)

ILLUSTRATIONS AND TEXT

The illustrations are an integral part of the course, and the text is closely related to them. The text is simple and brief, so that average and below average pupils are not discouraged by the sight of a solid page of print; even so, with some less able classes or pupils, teachers may find it appropriate to teach from the illustrations rather than from the text.

Inevitably, a course dealing with world faiths has to introduce a vocabulary of basic religious words and concepts, and when such words are first used they are emphasised and explained.

DISCUSSION QUESTIONS

Knowledge and understanding of the actions and beliefs of the major religions of the world is not simply a matter of instruction. It is essential that young people should be given the opportunity to think through the issues involved for themselves, and encouraged to think out what they believe about the fundamental questions of life to which religions offer answers: the purpose of human life, the problem of suffering and evil, the possibility of life after death, the existence of God, and so on. The discussion questions are not intended to be exhaustive, but to provide starters for discussion of the various issues raised in each unit.

Teachers will have their own preferred style of class discussion. It may be that the questions will lend themselves to discussion in small groups, followed by class discussion and individual written work.

FURTHER READING

More able classes, and brighter pupils in mixed-ability classes, will be able to go on to the suggestions for further reading provided at the back of the book. These, in the main, are readily available Religious Education textbooks, many of which will already be owned by R.E. teachers, and which if kept on an accessible shelf in the R.E. classroom, form the nucleus of an R.E. class library.

THINGS TO DO

After each section, suggestions are offered for further activities involving visits, talks, models, drawings, and creative written work. Some of the activities suggested will be easier for schools in cities, or at least within easy reach of the various religious communities referred to in the text. However, imaginative use of audio-visual aids, libraries, reference books and artefacts should enable all schools, however remote their setting, to tackle most of the activities.

CONSTRUCTING AN R.E. SYLLABUS

Each of the books in this course is complete in itself, and the books may be taken in any order. The number of themes tackled in one year will depend upon the number of periods per week allocated to Religious Education.

CHRISTIANITY AND OTHER WORLD FAITHS

Every effort has been made to look objectively at the main denominations of Christianity and at the major world religions found in Britain today — Hinduism, Judaism, Islam, and Sikhism. There are more units on Christianity than other religions simply because there are more manifestations of Christianity in present-day Britain than there are of other religions. One of the advantages of the recent revolution in Religious Education is that it is now possible, indeed acceptable and desirable, to teach much more about Christianity as a living faith than in the days when Agreed Syllabuses limited Religious Education to a study of the Bible.

Where there are clear similarities or common origins of certain features of different religions, these are indicated, but no attempt has been made to "compare" systematically one religion against another, or against some arbitrary norm. No assumption has been made of any particular faith-position on the part of the pupil or the teacher.

BRITAIN AND THE REST OF THE WORLD

Although the main emphasis of this course is on religion in Britain today, many units do focus on aspects of religions (including Christianity) in other parts of the world. This serves to heighten the pupils' awareness that religion is a world-wide phenomenon, and that all the religions being studied owe their origins to cultures, peoples and languages from beyond our shores.

ACKNOWLEDGEMENTS

I am most grateful to the following people, who have read all or part of the manuscript of this book and made many helpful comments and suggestions:
Tony Castle, Rabbi Douglas Charing, Ranchor Das, Dr. D.J. Drabu, Chris Lukey, David Melling, Daljit Singh, Sardar A.K. Singh, Revd. Michael Taylor, Peter Woodward, Mrs. Nina Taylor, and Susanne, my wife.

John Bailey

Contents

Page

RELIGIOUS BUILDINGS   9

1   Steeples and Towers   10
2   A Pentecostal Church   13
3   The Village Church   15
4   Inside an Anglican Church   16
5   A City Church   19
6   A Modern Church Building   21
7   A Methodist Church   22
8   A Baptist Church   25
9   A Medieval Cathedral   26
10   A Modern Cathedral   29
11   Eastern Orthodox Churches   31
12   A Roman Catholic Church   33
     Things to do   34
13   A Purpose-built Mosque   37
14   A House Converted to a Mosque   39
15   Inside a Mosque   41
16   The Ablutions Area   43
17   The Qur'an in Worship   45
18   A Synagogue   47
19   Inside a Synagogue   49
20   Features of a Synagogue   51
     Things to do   52
21   A Hindu Temple in London   54
22   Hindu Temples in India   57
23   A Sikh Gurdwara in Britain   59
24   The Golden Temple, Amritsar   61
     Things to do   63
25   A Quaker Meeting-House   65
26   A Mormon Temple   67
27   A House Church   68
     Things to do   70

Page

RELIGIOUS FESTIVALS   71

28   Christmas   73
29   Commercial Christmas   75
30   Shrove Tuesday   77
31   Easter   79
32   Whitsun   81
      Things to do   83
33   Ramadan   85
34   Eid-ul-Fitr   87
35   Eid-ul-Adha   89
36   Rosh Hashanah and Yom Kippur   90
37   Succoth   92
38   Hanukah and Purim   94
39   Pesach and Shavuot   96
      Things to do   98
40   Dussehra   101
41   Divali   103
42   Holi   105
43   The Birthday of Krishna   107
44   Baisakhi   108
45   The Birthday of Guru Nanak   111
      Things to do   113
46   Ancient Customs   115
47   New Year Celebrations   117
48   The Chinese New Year   119
49   A Flower Festival   121
50   A Harvest Festival   122
      Things to do   124
For further reading   125

Acknowledgements

The author and the publishers wish to thank the following for permission
to use copyright material:

British Tourist Authority: pp. 10, 18, 72, 76, 114, 120 (top), 122
Peter Lockwood: pp. 11, 12, 14 (foot), 16, 17, 20, 22, 24, 27, 28, 30 (foot), 38, 43, 46, 58,
    64, 66, 68, 80, 86 (foot), 123
Alan Hutchison Library Ltd.: pp. 14 (top), 26, 36, 41, 44 (foot), 84, 102, 104 (foot)
National Portrait Gallery: p. 23
Picturepoint – London: pp. 30 (top), 42 (top), 74, 78, 91, 116, 119
Ann and Bury Peerless: 40, 42 (foot), 44 (top), 54, 55, 56, 57, 60, 62, 63, 86 (top), 100, 101,
    103, 104 (top), 106, 108, 109, 110, 111, 112, 113
Jewish Education Bureau: pp. 48, 50, 90, 92, 93, 94, 96
The Trustees, The National Gallery, London: p. 82
Saudia/IPA Picture Library: p. 88
The Council of Christians and Jews: p. 95
Alan Liu: p. 118
Spring Colour Publications, Springfields, Spalding: p. 120 (foot)

Religious Buildings

This theme presents a review of the rich variety of churches, chapels, cathedrals, mosques, synagogues, temples and gurdwaras used for worship in Britain today. It looks at the symbolism of the design of these buildings, both inside and out, and examines how they are used. In passing and by way of contrast, notice is taken of some religious buildings in other lands.

Part of the skyline of Oxford

1 Steeples and Towers

How many churches can you see in the photograph of Oxford? (Look for towers or spires.) Many old towns have a number of churches. Some of these are *Parish* Churches — that is, they serve a particular area or parish. These are part of the Church of England, if the town is in England. Other churches belong to different *denominations* or branches of Christianity. They may be Roman Catholic or Nonconformist, such as Methodist, Baptist or United Reformed.

Years ago, when large numbers of people went to church regularly, all the churches in the picture would have been full to overflowing several times every Sunday. Nowadays, fewer people go to church, and many people have moved out of town and city centres, with the result that many church buildings are no longer needed. Sometimes, in towns and inner-city areas, you will find former churches being used for other purposes.

A former church now being used as a warehouse

FOR DISCUSSION

1   What is the church in the picture above now being used for? What changes do you think have taken place in the area, to cause the church to sell off the building?

2   Do you think it is true that fewer people go to church nowadays than in former times? If so, list some of the reasons for this.

3   In country areas, many small villages cannot afford the upkeep of their village church, and one priest or minister has to look after several villages. What difficulties and problems might this cause?

4   In some new towns and housing estates, churches have been built which serve a dual purpose: a place of worship on Sundays and a community centre during the week. What do you think of this idea? List some advantages and disadvantages.

2 A Pentecostal Church

Many towns in Britain have a bewildering array of different churches — Church of England, Roman Catholic, Methodist, United Reformed, Baptist, Salvation Army. Sometimes you may come across a church building which has changed hands recently. The church in the photograph was originally a Congregational Church, and when the Congregationalists united with the Presbyterians, they no longer needed the building, so it was sold to the Pentecostal Church.

Whereas most mainstream Christian churches in Britain are declining in membership, the Pentecostal church is growing. It is a lively, welcoming, informal church, with a firm belief in the truth of the Bible. Pentecostalists believe that true Christian conversion is being "born again" in the Holy Spirit of God, just as the disciples of Jesus experienced at the festival of Pentecost shortly after the first Easter. (See Acts of the Apostles, Chapter 2; see also Unit 32: Whitsun, and Unit 39: Pesach and Shavuot.)

As well as the various Christian churches, many towns and cities in Britain now have religious buildings of other faiths — Jewish synagogues, Muslim mosques, Sikh gurdwaras, and Hindu temples. Some of these are new and purpose-built; others may be converted churches or even large houses.

FOR DISCUSSION

1 Why are there so many different Christian churches? Some people in your class will probably go to church, or come from church-going families. How many different church backgrounds are represented in your class? Can you find out the main differences between them?

2 Why do you think the Congregational and Presbyterian Christians no longer needed the church building?

3 The fact that there are so many churches shows that people do like to meet together in large groups for worship. From your own experience, or from talking to your parents or other adults, make a list of the different activities that go on inside churches. Why is it necessary to have a special building for these activities?

◀ *A former Congregational church now being used by the Pentecostalists*

A village church — the parish church of St. Nicholas, Bathampton, Avon
Yew trees in the churchyard at Painswick, Gloucestershire

3   The Village Church

The top photograph shows a church at the heart of an English village. It is a typical country scene. The way in which the cottages cluster round the church in many villages seems to show that Christianity is central to the life of the people, as it undoubtedly was in the Middle Ages. The tower, pointing firmly heavenward, was a reminder of God, while at the same time providing our ancestors with a safe refuge in times of trouble. The gravestones around the church remind us that we must all die at some time, while the dark, evergreen yew trees found in so many churchyards may well be a symbol of eternal life. At one time, the longbows used by English archers were made from yew, and people were forbidden to cut down a fully-grown yew tree.

The photograph at the foot is of an avenue of yew trees in the churchyard at Painswick.

FOR DISCUSSION

1   Look at the pictures and identify the following features: tower, spire, gravestones, porch, yew trees. Why do you think so many churches have towers or spires? Why is it traditional for people to be buried in churchyards? Why are evergreens — yew, holly, mistletoe — so much a feature of traditional religion?

2   A common feature of many old churches today is the large, thermometer-type sign outside, saying something like "TWENTY THOUSAND POUNDS URGENTLY NEEDED TO REPAIR THIS CHURCH — PLEASE GIVE GENEROUSLY." Do you think it is right to spend money propping up church buildings, when millions of people in the world are starving? Is this a fair argument?

3   In some towns and cities it has been decided that some churches are worth preserving, whilst others should be demolished. But which ones should be preserved — those which are thought to be beautiful or those which are used regularly? If a beautiful old church ought to be saved, who should pay for it?

Looking towards the altar in a traditional Anglican church

4   Inside an Anglican Church

As you go into an Anglican (Church of England) church, you will probably notice a large, stone, basin-like object near the door. This is a *font*, which holds water and is used for baptisms. This particular font is of Saxon origin and you can see it has some very old carvings.

If you look towards the east end of the church, you will see a table,

A font

A pulpit

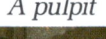

often covered by a richly-embroidered cloth and with a cross and candle-sticks standing on it. This is the *altar*, where the bread and wine are *consecrated* (blessed) at the communion service.

To the north side, there is usually a raised stand or platform, with steps leading up to it. This is the *pulpit*, from which the priest or minister preaches

An altar in a Church of England church

the sermon. The pulpit may be made of stone or wood. The one in the photograph is a wooden one mounted on a stone base.

On the opposite side of the church to the pulpit is a stand for the Bible. This is called a *lectern*. It may be a simple wooden stand, or it could be an ornate brass eagle with wings outspread, standing on a globe. This represents the Word of God being carried across the whole world.

FOR DISCUSSION

1 Why do you think the font is placed near the door of the church?

2 Why are many churches built so that the people facing the altar face East?

3 Most churches have an atmosphere of quietness and calm. Can you suggest a reason for this?

An eagle lectern

4 Even in the Church of England, there is a tremendous variety of interior furnishings and decorations. Some are very plain, some very ornate. Why do you think this is? Which do you prefer?

5   A City Church

"Sir Christopher Wren
   Said to some men,
   'If anyone calls,
   Tell him I'm designing St. Paul's.'"

Many churches and cathedrals were designed in the plan of a cross. Another religious symbol used widely in architecture is the circle — symbol of perfection and completeness. Many classical Roman temples were round, topped with domes, and when the Greek and Roman writers and philosophers were rediscovered during the fifteenth, sixteenth and seventeenth centuries, their art and designs were re-created, too. This period is called the *Renaissance* (rebirth), and Sir Christopher Wren's famous dome and drum of St. Paul's Cathedral, London, is a "rebirth" of a Roman temple.

This photograph in a way symbolises the developments of the twentieth century. The London skyline was once dominated by the dome of St. Paul's. Now the cathedral is surrounded by the towering office blocks, memorials to commerce, technology and materialism. Yet the cathedral still stands, in the heart of the city; a constant reminder of man's belief in the presence of God in the world.

FOR DISCUSSION

1   Why is the circle an appropriate symbol for God?

2   The previous Cathedral of St. Paul's was partly destroyed by the Great Fire of London in 1666. Christopher Wren was asked to design the new City of London. His design — which, apart from St. Paul's itself, was never carried out — had the Cathedral at the hub, with roads leading out like the spokes of a wheel. Why do you think he put the Cathedral at the centre?

3   Nowadays, when a city centre or town centre is redesigned, great care is often taken to preserve and emphasise the ancient cathedral or town church. Why do you think this is, when so few people actually go to church, and city centre churches are often empty on Sundays? Is it the result of sentiment, superstition, deep-down feelings of guilt, appreciation of beauty and architectural worth, or hard-headed business — the need to attract tourists? Or could it be that town planners and city fathers really do want to bring back Christianity to the centre of life?

19

◀ *St. Paul's Cathedral, London*

A modern church from the outside

Inside the same modern church

6 A Modern Church Building

Sometimes, it is hard to tell from the outside of a modern church building that it *is* a church. But there are usually some clues. Even if there is no tower or spire, there will probably be some feature which indicates that it is a church — for instance, a cross. Sometimes there are stained-glass windows, and invariably there is a notice-board outside, giving the name of the church, the name of the vicar or minister, and the times of services.

When you go inside, the layout of a modern church may be different from that of a traditional church. The main features are still there — altar, pulpit, lectern, and so on — but the altar is sometimes central, so that the priest can stand behind it, facing the congregation, rather than standing with his back to them. And the chairs or pews for the people may be arranged around the altar, in a semicircle or on three sides of a square, so that the impression is given of a family sitting round a table.

You will also notice that most of the furniture and fittings, including the works of art, and the windows, candlesticks and crosses, are more likely to be modern rather than old-fashioned. There may be an electronic organ instead of a pipe organ, and if you look at one of the prayer books stacked at the back waiting to be given out, you may well find that it is written in modern, everyday English, not in the traditional style.

FOR DISCUSSION

1 Many older people who have been going to church all their lives dislike modern churches. Why do you think this is?

2 Why do you think some modern churches are so plain and simple, compared with the painstaking detail of medieval churches?

3 Do you prefer the modern, abstract art you often see in modern church buildings to the statues and paintings of saints and apostles you find in many older churches? Do you think people who go to church notice things like this, and choose which church to go to? Or do they go to the nearest church, or the one they have always been to?

The view from the gallery of Linthwaite Methodist Church, West Yorkshire

7   A Methodist Church

If you compare this picture, showing the interior of a typical Methodist church, with, say, the picture of the inside of an Anglican church, the main difference is that instead of the altar being the focal point, in a Methodist church the pulpit is the dominant feature. This symbolises what is probably the most important difference in the forms of worship used in these two churches. The central feature of Church of England worship is the sharing of the bread and wine in the *Eucharist,* or Communion Service; the central feature of Methodist worship is the preaching of the Word of God, the sermon.

John Wesley, the founder of Methodism, was a Church of England parson who, in 1738, had a deep religious experience of the saving love of God, which he wanted to share with others. He travelled widely, preaching in the open air, and when his followers began to build or adapt places to meet in for worship, they naturally made the sermon the centrepiece of their service, and the pulpit became the central feature of their chapels.

John Wesley preaching

FOR DISCUSSION

1 If you can, go to a Methodist church service, or ask someone who has been to tell you about it. Did you, or did they, find it easy to sit through a thirty- or forty-minute sermon? Do you think people used to be able to concentrate better in the eighteenth and nineteenth centuries, before the development of television? Do you think the Methodist church should use other means of communication, or is it more important to keep the sermon as a link with the past?

2 Since 1956, the Methodists have been in conversation with the Church of England about uniting the two churches. In 1982, the Church of England General Synod (the governing body) voted narrowly against proposals for a Covenant of Unity. Why do you think it is taking so long for these two churches, which have so much in common, to unite? What are the main differences which are keeping them apart?

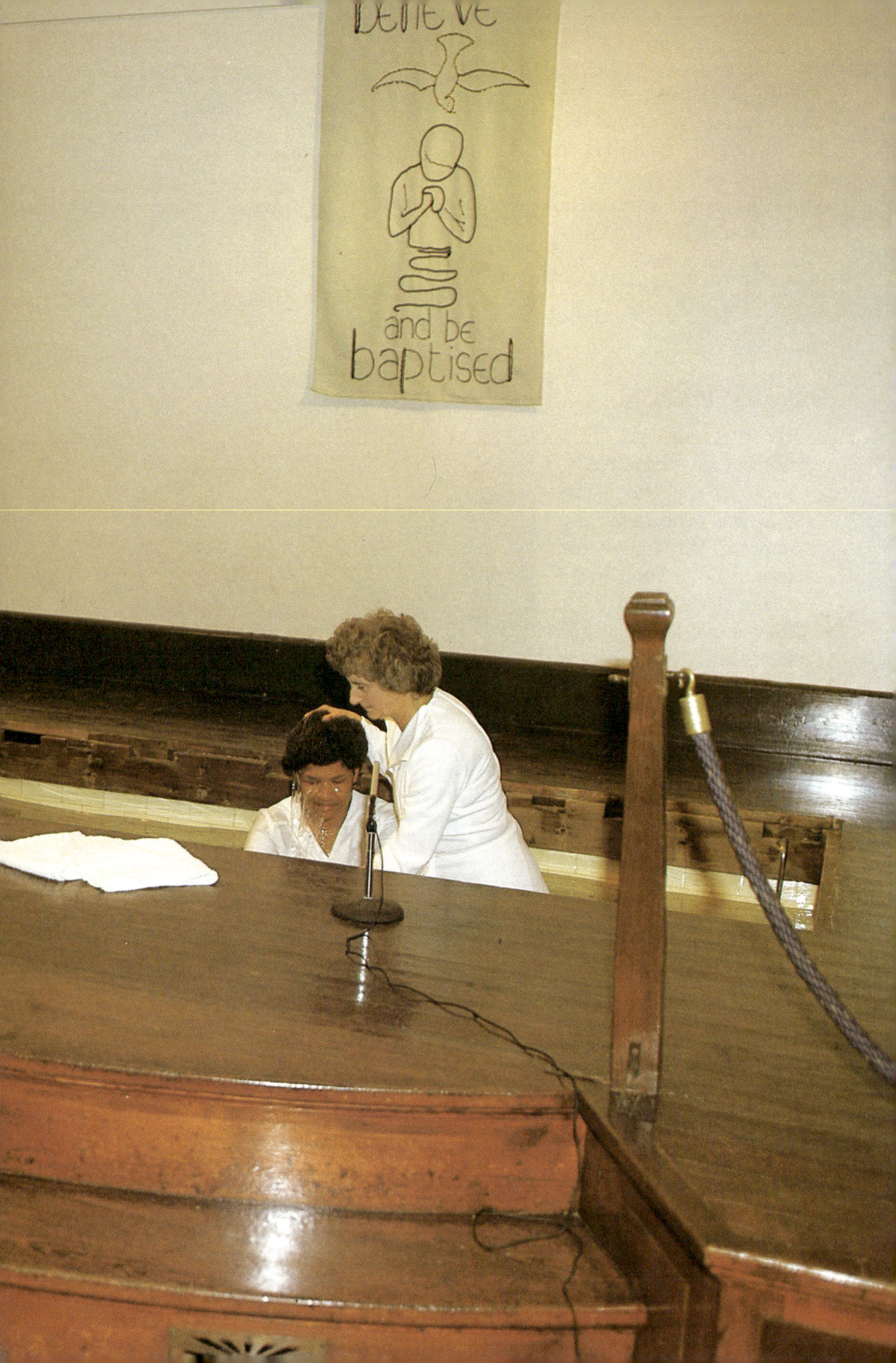

8   A Baptist Church

Just as the pulpit placed centrally in a Methodist church emphasises the importance of the sermon, so in a Baptist church there is a
central feature which is very important to Baptists. This is the
baptistery, or pool.

Baptists believe that you should be baptised only when you are old
enough to know what you are committing yourself to. This is known
as Believer's Baptism.

When a baptism takes place in a Baptist church, the person being
baptised usually gives a public testimony, or statement, of his or her
faith. He or she wears white clothes, and the minister may put on a
pair of waders. They go down the steps into the pool, and the
minister ducks the candidate right under the water, baptising him or
her in the name of Jesus Christ. The newly-baptised person then goes
to change into dry clothes, and the service continues.

Of course, the pool is usually kept empty and covered, to guard
against accidental immersions!

FOR DISCUSSION

1   Do you agree with the Baptist view that people should be baptised
     only when they are old enough to know what they are doing?
     What do you think the minimum age should be?

2   If you were being admitted to membership of a club or a religious
     group, do you think you would be able to stand up in front of
     everybody and give a testimony about what you believed? Do you
     think this is a good test of readiness for membership?

◀ *The minister baptising a candidate*

Lincoln Cathedral

9   A Medieval Cathedral

You can just imagine what the tourist guide would say about this building! "The great Minster Cathedral of Lincoln sits proudly above the ancient city, visible from over thirty kilometres away, as befits the seat of a Bishop whose *diocese* (area) once covered half of England." Well, the guide book would be right: Lincoln Cathedral *is* an incredible sight, and the sheer size and splendour of the building shows just how powerful and wealthy the Church of England used to be.

Bishops were great landowners and could, if they wished, live like princes. But we must not overlook the vision and determination of a man like Bishop Remigius of Lincoln, who started the building of Lincoln Cathedral to the glory of God; or the humility and concern of Hugh, Bishop of Lincoln in the twelfth century, whose love for his

St. Hugh's tomb in the Angel Choir of Lincoln Cathedral

people was so great that after his death he was made a saint. The East End of Lincoln Cathedral, called the "Angel Choir" (because of the carvings of angels on the walls), was built to house the tomb of St. Hugh. This became a centre for pilgrims from all over the country, and the stone step at the foot of the tomb is worn hollow by the knees of generations of pilgrims.

FOR DISCUSSION

1   A splendid building like Lincoln Cathedral must have cost an immense amount of money to build. Why do you think the people of the time spent so much on a place of worship? Do you think the ordinary townspeople of Lincoln would have grumbled about the expense, or would they have been glad of the extra work, and proud of the finished result? Have attitudes changed today?

2   Do you think the medieval bishops, living grandly in their rich palaces, ever felt guilty about the contrast between their life-style and that of the peasants? Do you think they saw any conflict between the teachings of Christ and the wealth of the church? Why do you think some bishops, such as Hugh, were so different? Are bishops and clergy wealthy and powerful today? What has brought about the change?

3   Why do Christians make pilgrimages to places such as Lincoln and Canterbury? What other places of pilgrimage, both Christian and non-Christian, can you think of?
    (Book 4 in this series deals with pilgrimage in more detail.)

Liverpool's Roman Catholic Cathedral at the northern end of Hope Street

The tower of the Anglican Cathedral beyond the southern end of Hope Street

10 A Modern Cathedral

The Roman Catholic Cathedral of Christ the King in Liverpool was consecrated in May 1967. When the Roman Catholic Archbishop of Liverpool invited architects to submit designs for the new cathedral, he specified a building which could seat between two and three thousand people, all of whom should be able to see the altar and with no one sitting more than twenty-three metres away from it. Frederick Gibberd's winning design met these requirements by having a circular plan, with a central altar. As you can see, from a distance the building looks like a huge tent, with a massive crown on top, symbolising the Crown of Thorns placed on the head of Jesus at the Crucifixion.

Just a few hundred metres away from the Roman Catholic Cathedral stands the Anglican Cathedral, a vast, stone building, begun in 1904 and consecrated in 1924. This is in the Gothic style, to a design by Gilbert Scott.

The road which connects these two twentieth-century cathedrals is called Hope Street. This has become a symbol to many Christians that one day the different branches of the Christian Church will come together in unity.

FOR DISCUSSION

1 Why are cathedrals still being built today? Why do we need large, central places of worship, when there are plenty of local churches? Do you think new cathedrals should be built in the best "modern" style, like the Catholic Cathedral in Liverpool, or in a "traditional" style?

2 Do you think it is right for churches to spend so much money on new buildings, when there is so much poverty and suffering in the world? Ancient churches and cathedrals were built "to the glory of God"; is this still true today?

3 Do you think the linking by Hope Street of the two cathedrals in Liverpool should be viewed as a symbol of hope, that one day the churches will overcome their differences? Or do you see it as a symbol of despair, because they are still divided?

The iconostasis reflects the many lights in this Orthodox church
The Russian Orthodox Cathedral in Kensington

11 Eastern Orthodox Churches

The great *Schism*, or split, in the Christian church took place in 1054 C.E. There was a formal split between the Pope of Rome and the Patriarch of Constantinople which led to the two main branches of Christianity — the Catholic church in the West and the Orthodox churches in the East.

A distinctive feature of all Eastern Orthodox churches is the *iconostasis*, which means "place of the icons, or pictures". This is a screen which divides the main body of the church from the inner sanctuary, and it is usually covered with icons.

Icons are religious pictures of Jesus, scenes such as the Crucifixion, or saints such as Peter or John, or Mary, the mother of Jesus. Their purpose is to remind the worshipper that in worshipping God, they are joining with the saints in Heaven.

The iconostasis screen stands for the separation between Heaven and Earth. It has a door which is opened at several points during the Communion service, revealing the altar table, to show that in the person of Jesus, God has ended that separation.

There are many independent Orthodox churches, each based on a particular country, e.g. Greek, Serbian (Yugoslavian), Russian, Syrian. There is a Russian Orthodox cathedral in Kensington, London. Its bishop is Metropolitan Anthony Bloom. In the Russian Orthodox Church, a bishop is in charge of a diocese and a metropolitan is in charge of a whole province. Metropolitan Anthony is Metropolitan of Sourozh, which is the province of Great Britain and Ireland and has about 250 000 members.

FOR DISCUSSION

1 On entering an Orthodox church, a believer will usually light a candle in front of an icon. Why do you think this is?

2 What features of the Russian cathedral in London suggest to you that this is not an Anglican or a Roman Catholic cathedral?

3 Find photographs of as many Eastern Orthodox churches as you can in reference books. What similarities and differences do you notice between them and other Christian churches?

12 A Roman Catholic Church

Many people forget that until the Reformation, Britain was a Catholic Christian country. Many old churches and cathedrals, now Church of England, were originally founded as Catholic churches. After Henry VIII, there were many years of violence between Catholics and Protestants. Not until this century did the Anglican Church and the Roman Catholic Church start talking seriously again about the possibility of union.

Given this common background, it is not surprising that Anglican churches and Catholic churches are very similar, both outside and in. The main difference you will notice is that a Roman Catholic church is likely to have more images and statues, particularly of the Blessed Virgin Mary, the mother of Jesus, and of the Stations of the Cross, representations of the various incidents which took place when Jesus was carrying his cross to the place of execution. Sometimes the Catholic church will be lavishly decorated, as is the one at Ottobeuren, in West Germany.

The Abbey Church of Ottobeuren is in a part of Southern Germany known as Schwabia, where there are many churches in this baroque style. This is a style of architecture, dating from the seventeenth and eighteenth centuries, which uses such a great variety of art and sculpture that the structure of the building is almost hidden.

FOR DISCUSSION

1 Listen to music by some of the great composers of the seventeenth and eighteenth centuries, such as Vivaldi, Bach, Mozart and Handel. Do you think their music has anything in common with baroque architecture? Choose a piece of music by one of these composers which you think would be suitable for a performance in the Abbey Church of Ottobeuren.

2 In terms of regular church attendance, the biggest single Christian denomination in England is not the Church of England but the Roman Catholic Church. Can you think of any reasons for this?

◀ *Inside the Roman Catholic Abbey Church of Ottobeuren*

Things to do — Christian Churches

1 Make a large chart, with Christian Churches along one axis and Features of a Christian Church along the other.

Christian Churches

Features	Eastern Orthodox	Roman Catholic	Church of England	Methodist	etc.
Altar					
Pulpit					
Lectern					
Font					
Iconostasis					
Baptism tank					
etc.					

Tick the appropriate column and space to show which Church usually contains which features. Which Church has most features? Which has least?

2 Make a sketch map of your village, town or district. Mark in the different churches, chapels, etc. (use a different symbol for the different churches).

Shade in on the map where most people live — new housing estates, blocks of flats, and so on. Are the churches situated conveniently close to where people live? If not, why not? What changes have taken place which mean the churches are badly situated?

3 Choose one particular church in your neighbourhood. Find out all you can about the building — who designed it, when it was built, how much it cost, what changes have been made to it, and so on.

If possible, take photographs of the church, both inside and out, or make drawings which illustrate interesting features of the building. Arrange your work on a large piece of sugar paper so that it can be put on display in the classroom.

4   Working in groups or as a class, devise a questionnaire to investigate how often people go to church or to some other place of worship in your locality. These are the sort of questions to ask:

Do you go to church or other place of worship regularly?
Yes/No.

How often do you go to church or other place of worship?
Occasionally/Once a year/Once a month/Weekly/More often.

Which church or place of worship do you attend?
Church of England, Roman Catholic, Nonconformist,
Other Christian, Hindu, Sikh, Jewish, Muslim,
Other (specify).

With the help of your teacher, you should be able to make up a questionnaire which will give you a good picture of the church-going habits of your neighbourhood. Decide how many people you will need to interview to make a representative sample. Go out and do the interviews — take the advice of your parents and teacher about how to contact people to interview, and how to conduct the interviews.

When the whole class has brought back a reasonable number of completed questionnaires, discuss the best way of analysing your results and presenting your conclusions. Your Maths teacher will be able to give you some advice about this.

5   Imagine you are an architect and you have been asked to design a multi-purpose church/community centre for a new housing estate. Make a list of all the basic activities which the building will be used for, and plan a building which meets these needs.

All the examples produced by the class could be put on display, and a panel of experts — clergymen, architects, community workers — could be invited to judge them.

Sometimes an architect who is entering a design for a competition will make a model of it, so that the judges can "see" the project more clearly. You may like to make a model of your own design.

Regent's Park Mosque, showing the golden dome, minaret and colonnade

13   A Purpose-built Mosque

Most people would recognise immediately that the building in the photograph is a *mosque*; the dome and the tall, slender tower — the *minaret* — are quite distinctive. Some people would be quite surprised, however, to learn that this beautiful mosque is in the heart of London, close to Regent's Park. It is called Regent's Park Mosque.

The word mosque comes from an Arabic word meaning "to bow down", and a mosque is a place where Muslims meet to bow in worship before Allah (their name for God).

The dome of a mosque symbolises the universe. It marks the building as a mosque, in much the same way that a tower or spire signifies a Christian church. The dome also has a practical purpose — it helps to keep the interior of the building cool, which is very important in hot regions such as Arabia, where the religion of Islam began. It also acts as a sounding-chamber to amplify the voice of the *imam* (religious leader) when he leads the worship and preaches the sermon.

The slender minaret also has a practical use. A man called a *muezzin* (caller to prayer) goes up to the little balcony near the top of the minaret and walks round it, calling the faithful to prayer. This happens five times a day, and it is important because the times of prayer change according to the season. Nowadays, of course, the voice of the muezzin may be broadcast from a loudspeaker at the top of the minaret, and the call to prayer may be pre-recorded. The call to prayer serves the same function as the bells of a Christian church, which are rung on Sundays before the services.

FOR DISCUSSION

1 Most religions try to make their places of worship beautiful, and use symbols in the design of the buildings — spires pointing upwards, over-arching domes, circles and spheres. Why do you think this is? Can you see any similarities between the Regent's Park Mosque and St. Paul's Cathedral?

2 How practical is the call to prayer today, in the heart of a modern city? Why is the tradition continued? Can you see any difficulties for a Muslim in Britain today, trying to obey the call to prayer at work or at school?

14 A House Converted to a Mosque

Not all mosques are beautiful, purpose-built structures with golden domes. Many mosques are simple, plain buildings, and in Britain they are often converted houses near the centres of towns or cities.

Sometimes, other old buildings such as churches, shops or vicarages are bought and converted into mosques. When this is done, Muslims usually try to make some small changes to the style of the building to show that it is now a mosque. For example, a small artificial dome may be added above the doorway, or the windows and doorways may be given Islamic arches. Converted houses may have some Arabic writing from the Qur'an (the holy book of Islam) placed in the window or above the door, as in this photograph.

FOR DISCUSSION

1 Where would you expect to find buildings which have been converted to mosques? Why do you think so few external structural changes are made to such buildings?

2 Discuss the shift in population which could bring about the change of use of a building from a church to a synagogue to a mosque. Over what period of time would this have happened? What does a change like this tell us about the changing fortunes of these racial and religious groups?

◀ *A house converted to a mosque*

The mihrab and minbar in a mosque at Mandu, India

Muslims worshipping in front of the mihrab of a mosque in Old Delhi, India

15 Inside a Mosque

When you first go inside a mosque, it comes as something of a surprise to see how plain it is — no statues or pictures, no chairs or pews, no altar. There are, however, some features which you will always find inside a mosque. The first of these is the *mihrab*, a semicircular niche or recess in one of the walls. This indicates the direction of Mecca, the Muslim holy city. The worshippers in a mosque must face Mecca to worship, so the mihrab is very important. Sometimes the carpet has parallel lines marked on it.

Another feature usually found in a mosque is a *minbar*, a pulpit with steps, from which the imam delivers his sermon at the midday worship on a Friday.

Images and statues are not allowed in mosques but many of them do have very beautiful decorations. These can take the form of graceful and ornate arches and geometric designs often incorporating passages from the Qur'an in Arabic script.

Decorations in a mosque at Isfahan, Iran

FOR DISCUSSION

1 Why do you think images are not allowed in a mosque?

2 The floor of a mosque is usually covered with a carpet. Why do you suppose this is? This carpet often has a series of parallel lines marked on it. What do you think these are for?

Muslims at the fountain of a mosque courtyard in Morocco
Muslims in the ablutions area of a mosque in Old Delhi

16 The Ablutions Area

Before praying, either at home or in the mosque, the Muslim must prepare for this by ritual washing, called *wudu*. The way this should be done is laid down in the Qur'an. It involves washing the hands, the mouth and throat (by gargling), the nose and face, the arms, the head, the ears and the feet. Cold water is often used, which also has the practical effect of waking you up — and cooling you down.

In hot countries, the mosque will usually have a courtyard with a fountain or a pool where the wudu may be performed.

In Britain, mosques are usually provided with a shoe-rack, where shoes may be left, and there is also a row of wash-basins for the ablutions. This photograph shows a shoe-rack in a mosque at Keighley in West Yorkshire. The rack would be full of shoes on a Friday, but, of course, no photographs are allowed to be taken then.

A shoe-rack in a mosque in Britain

FOR DISCUSSION

1 Why is it so important for Muslims to be ritually clean before worship?

2 It used to be the custom in Britain to wear your best clothes to go to church — "Sunday best". Do you think this is in any way similar to the Muslim principle of wudu?

3 Water seems to play a very important part in many religions. How many examples of the ritual use of water in religions can you think of?

A boy reading the Qur'an in the Mahabat Khan Mosque

A decorated medieval manuscript of the Qur'an

17 The Qur'an in Worship

The Qur'an, the holy book of Islam, written in Arabic, is available for believers to read at any time in the mosque. The Muslim will wash his or her hands before touching the Qur'an, which must be placed somewhere clean, usually on a special, low stand. The believer then sits cross-legged before it and reads aloud.

This boy is reading the Qur'an in the Mahabat Khan Mosque at Peshawar, in Pakistan.

The prayers which are recited during the midday *salat* (act of worship) in the mosque are based on the Qur'an, and the sermon given by the imam on a Friday consists of an explanation of a passage from the Qur'an, together with teaching about everyday life.

Many Muslims learn the Qur'an off by heart so that they can recite it and live their whole life by it. A person who can do this is called a *hafiz*.

FOR DISCUSSION

1 Why do you think the Qur'an is treated with so much respect by Muslims?

2 All Muslims learn Arabic so that they can read the Qur'an in its original language. Why do you think this is so important?

3 The Qur'an is supposed to be treated with great reverence, and no other book should be placed upon it or above it. Discuss where you would keep a Qur'an if one were given to the school for the R.E. department. Could the place where the Qur'an is kept cause offence to any other religion? How could this be resolved?

4 Do you know anyone who can recite parts of the Qur'an, or the Bible, or any other holy book, by heart? How did they set about learning it? What is the advantage of knowing your holy book by heart?

18   A Synagogue

The word "synagogue" comes from the Greek word for a meeting or assembly. References to synagogues go back to the time when the Jewish people were in exile in Babylon, 2500 years ago. They needed somewhere to meet for worship, to keep their religion alive.

You would probably be able to tell from the outside that this building is a synagogue. The writing over the doorway does not look like English. It is, in fact, Hebrew, the ancient language of the Jewish people. Many synagogues also have on the outside a Star of David, which has come to be a symbol of Judaism. Another Jewish symbol, which you might see in a stained-glass window, is the seven-branched candlestick or *menorah*. This reminds Jews of the menorah which used to stand in the Temple in Jerusalem, destroyed by the Romans in the first century C.E.

Very few early synagogues survive today. Apart from the ravages of time, most synagogues in Israel were destroyed by the various people who have occupied the land, from the Greeks and the Romans to the present day. This photograph shows the remains, partly rebuilt, of a second-century synagogue at Capernaum, near the Sea of Galilee.

The partly-restored second-century synagogue at Capernaum

FOR DISCUSSION

1   Why is it so important for people in exile in a strange land to have somewhere to meet for worship?

2   Why do you think the Greeks and the Romans who occupied Israel destroyed the synagogues of the Jewish people?

◀ *A synagogue in South Manchester*

Inside a synagogue, looking towards the Ark
A good view of the gallery inside a modern synagogue

19 Inside a Synagogue

Like most Orthodox synagogues, this one is rectangular, with seats on three sides, facing inwards. The fourth side, the one nearest Jerusalem, contains the *Ark*, a recessed cupboard which holds the scrolls of the Hebrew bible.

There are two main divisions of Judaism in Britain today — Orthodox and Reform. The Orthodox Jews are very traditional. They try to keep to the form of worship which has been used for centuries, and their services are conducted in Hebrew. In an Orthodox synagogue, men and women sit separately. The women sit upstairs in the *gallery*, which you can see in the picture. Orthodox Jews also try to obey the laws given in the *Torah*, the first five books of the Bible. For example, they would not drive a car on the Sabbath, as that would be working. So an Orthodox Jew would walk to the synagogue on the Sabbath.

In a Reform synagogue, by contrast, men and women sit together, and part of the service is conducted in the language of the country.

FOR DISCUSSION

1 Why do you think synagogues are built so that one end is in the direction of Jerusalem?

2 Can you think of any reasons why men and women should sit separately in a service of worship? Why do you think this is so important to Orthodox Jews?

3 Many of the laws of Judaism are very difficult to carry out literally in today's world, which no doubt is why Reform Jews do not try to obey all of them. Do you think it is better to modify the laws openly, as Reform Jews do, or to try to obey all the laws but break some of them if you have to, as many Orthodox Jews do?

The scrolls, visible through the open doors of the Ark, in a modern synagogue

The bimah in a modern synagogue

20   Features of a Synagogue

The focal point of a synagogue is the *Ark*, containing the scrolls of the Torah, the first five books of the Jewish Bible. Torah means "teaching", and the laws of the Torah teach the Jewish people how they should live. The scrolls are long rolls of parchment, attached to two wooden rollers, one at each end. The wooden rollers are usually capped with silver crowns. When the scrolls are rolled up, they are covered with an embroidered velvet cloth and a silver shield, rather like a large napkin ring. This is a reminder of the breastplate which used to be worn by the High Priest in the Temple in Jerusalem.

The doors of the Ark are often covered by a curtain, and on either side of the Ark you may find the Ten Commandments in Hebrew. These are usually on two plaques, which stand for the two tablets of stone on which, according to the Torah, the commandments were originally given to Moses by God. (See Exodus, Chapter 31, verse 18.) Hanging above the Ark is an everlasting light, a reminder of the seven-branched menorah which used to burn in the Temple.

In the centre of the synagogue is a raised platform, with railings and a reading-desk. This is called the *bimah*. When the scrolls are taken out of the Ark during the Sabbath service, they are paraded round the synagogue and brought to the bimah to be opened and a portion read to the congregation. There are some seats in front of the bimah, facing the Ark, where the elders or wardens of the congregation sit during the service.

FOR DISCUSSION

1   When the Ten Commandments were originally given to Moses, they were kept in an Ark which was a wooden chest with carrying-poles. (See Exodus, Chapter 25, verses 10–22.) Why did this chest need to be portable? When and why did the chest become a built-in cupboard?

2   The Torah is also known as the Tree of Life. Why do you think this is?

3   Can you think of any features of a Christian church which originate from the Jewish synagogue?

Things to do — Mosques and Synagogues

1 If at all possible, arrange to visit a mosque. Remember that you will have to take off your shoes, and cover your head. Muslims usually wear a special prayer-hat, but any form of head-covering — even a clean handkerchief — will do. Make a list of all the things you notice: dome, minaret, shoe-rack, wash-basins, carpet, Qur'an stand, mihrab, minbar, etc. Write a few notes of description, or do a sketch, for each.

When you get back to school, make a class drawing or cardboard model of the mosque, working in groups, each group contributing one item. If it is a model, it could have a removable roof so that the interior can be examined. When you have completed the model, position it so that the mihrab is towards Mecca. (If it is a drawing, include a plan and put the direction of Mecca on the plan.)

Decorate your model or drawing with geometrical designs and calligraphy (handwriting) from the Qur'an.

2 Choose a passage from a holy book — the Bible, the Qur'an, the Torah, the Guru Granth Sahib — and learn it by heart. It would be very impressive if you could learn it in the original language, but it may mean more to you if you learn it in English, unless you also speak the original language! Ask the advice of your parents, your priest (if you belong to a religious group) or your teacher, before choosing a passage to learn.

3 Imagine you are a Muslim, and you have recently come to Britain from Pakistan (a Muslim country). You are finding everything strange and different — the weather, the school, the food, the apparent lack of respect for religion, the different attitude of boys towards girls. Above all, you find it difficult to get used to the fact that the mosque is some distance away, and is a converted terrace house in a town. Write to your family in Pakistan about your experiences.

4 Imagine you are a builder, and you have been called in by the local Muslim community to help them with the conversion of a house into a mosque. Make a list of all the work that would have to be done, both artistic (e.g. changing the design of the windows)

and functional (e.g. putting in wash-basins). Make a detailed drawing of a large house with all your design changes shown.

5   Make a model scroll. You will need two short pieces of wood or thin cardboard tubes, and a long roll of paper. Write out a passage from the Torah on your scroll. You might choose one of the central parts such as the Ten Commandments (Exodus, Chapter 20, verses 1–17) or one of the well-known stories, such as Adam and Eve (Genesis, Chapter 2, verses 5–24). Make a bag to keep the scroll in — red velvet would be ideal — and make a crown and breastplate out of silver-painted cardboard.

6   Visit a synagogue and see how many of the features described in this book you can find. Make a large drawing of the East Wall, containing the Ark, copying as accurately as you can the Hebrew lettering of the Ten Commandments. (If you are not able to visit a synagogue, use the photographs in this book to give you some ideas for your drawing.)

7   Imagine you are a Russian Jew, driven out of your country by the cruel *pogroms* (massacres) at the beginning of the twentieth century and newly arrived in Britain. You find a group of fellow Jews, in a northern city (say Leeds or Manchester) who, despite their own poverty, make you welcome. Write a letter to your family and friends back home, describing your experiences.

8   A classroom can make a very good "model" synagogue — particularly if it has a sliding blackboard with a cupboard behind it which can represent the Ark. Turn the classroom into a synagogue. How will you represent the bimah? The Ark? Using the model scrolls, act out that part of the service when the scrolls are removed from the Ark and brought to the bimah to be read.

9   In the past, Jewish communities have bought unwanted churches and converted them into synagogues. Methodist or Congregational churches with balconies were particularly suitable for this purpose. Make a list of all the items of furniture which the Church authorities would probably remove before the building was sold, and a list of the changes, both inside and outside, which the Jewish community would make to the building before it could be used as a synagogue.

The Radha Krishna Temple, London

21 A Hindu Temple in London

Mosques and synagogues are basically meeting-places where worship takes place. The origin of the Hindu temple is quite different. It was traditionally the home of a god, and only later did it become a meeting-place for worship. Every Hindu temple has some sort of representation of a god, usually a statue, with a canopy or covering over it as a mark of respect.

The temple in the photograph above is the Radha Krishna temple in Balham High Road, London, and the idol in the shrine represents Krishna, an incarnation or birth of the supreme god, Vishnu. The people have come to pay their respects to the god; they will probably have brought gifts of flowers or food. In the photograph on page 55, priests in a Hindu temple in South India are accepting food on behalf of the gods.

Most temples also have an attendant or a priest, who looks after the statue of the god and gives people who visit the shrine a gift from the

Hindu priests accepting the ritual food on behalf of the gods

god, called *prasad*. This is usually sweet food. The lady who runs the Radha Krishna Temple is known as Mother Shyama. You can see her picture on the left of the photograph on page 54.

FOR DISCUSSION

1 Some people think that Hindus worship the statue of the god at a shrine, and call this idolatry. What do you think? Is it in fact any different from having statues of the Blessed Virgin Mary in a Catholic church, or icons of Jesus in an Orthodox church?

2 Why do you think some religions love to represent their god or gods in statues and paintings, and others, notably Judaism and Islam, absolutely forbid it? Which do you find more helpful — to have an image of God in human form, or to have no picture of God? What are the advantages and disadvantages of each?

3 What do you think of the Hindu custom of giving prasad to visitors to the temple? What are your childhood memories of being taken to a place of worship when you were young?

22 Hindu Temples in India

Most Hindu temples in Britain are converted churches, church halls or houses, and the canopy which covers the statue of the god is inside the building. But in India there are many temples which are built just to house the statue, and the elaborate roof is itself the canopy over the god.

The photograph shows the temple at Kanchipuram in southern India. The carved tower is the canopy over the statue of the god, Siva. It represents a mountain. In many ancient religions, mountains were thought to be sacred, perhaps because they reach up to the sky and were thought to be the homes of the gods.

The carvings on these temple roofs or towers are detailed and intricate. This is a close-up of a sculpture on the twelfth-century Hoysala Temple at Halebid, in Mysore, India. It shows the god Siva dancing on a demon. There are three gods widely worshipped in Hinduism today: Brahma, the creator; Vishnu, the preserver, who came to earth in many forms (including that of Krishna, as we have seen), to help mankind; and Siva, the destroyer, who also brings new life. These three gods together are called the *Trimurti*; many Hindus see them as three forms of the one god.

A sculpture of Siva dancing

FOR DISCUSSION

1 Can you think of any stories or myths which connect God or the gods with high mountains?

2 Think of the way in which Nature renews itself — plants grow, flower, seed, and die, then grow again. Scientists tell us that animals and plants depend upon each other in a close relationship. Does the Hindu belief in Brahma the creator, Vishnu the preserver, and Siva the Destroyer, contradict the scientific view of the world, or could it be seen as a poetic way of saying the same thing?

◀ *The Siva Temple at Kanchipuram in southern India*

A purpose-built gurdwara in Huddersfield, West Yorkshire

Inside the same gurdwara

23 A Sikh Gurdwara in Britain

A Sikh place of worship is called a *gurdwara*, and it has one distinguishing feature from the outside: the *nishan sahib*, or Sikh religious and national flag. This serves a similar purpose to a church steeple, or the minaret on a mosque — it guides the worshipper to the place of worship. Gurdwara means "the door or house of the Guru". In Sikh religious language, Guru means spiritual teacher or guide.

When Guru Gobind Singh, the tenth and last Sikh Guru, was about to die, he decreed that the Sikh Holy Scripture should from then on be their Guru, and it became the *Guru Granth Sahib*.

There are gurdwaras in most of Britain's major cities. When you go inside a gurdwara, the most striking feature is the *palki,* or canopy, over the place where the Guru Granth Sahib is kept during the day.

The Guru Granth Sahib is placed on a specially designed wooden stool, on a raised platform called a *takht*. The reader sits cross-legged on the takht behind the Guru Granth Sahib, and a *chauri*, a whisk of animal hair which is a symbol of regal dignity, is waved over the Guru Granth Sahib as a mark of respect.

The gurdwara has no chairs. Worshippers sit cross-legged on the floor, facing the Guru Granth Sahib. This emphasises the importance of the Guru Granth Sahib; on its raised takht and stool, it is above everyone else and reminds Sikhs of one of their basic beliefs — that everyone, whatever his or her caste (class) or position, is equal before God.

FOR DISCUSSION

1 A Sikh gurdwara is a house or room for a book. Why is the Guru Granth Sahib so special for the Sikhs? Does it strike you as strange that people should regard a book as a living teacher, or can you think of other examples where a book is so influential that it could be said to "live"?

2 Do you like the Sikh idea of all people being equal before God? Can you think of religions in which this has not always been true, or religious buildings whose furniture highlights the differences in status rather than emphasises equality?

24 The Golden Temple, Amritsar

The fifth Guru of the Sikhs, Guru Arjan, was the religious teacher at a time when the Sikh community in the Punjab was becoming prosperous. He made a beautiful artificial lake at Amritsar, in the Punjab, in northern India, and on an island in the centre he built a Sikh gurdwara, known as the Golden Temple of Amritsar. It is not a towering building, symbolising a mountain, like a Hindu temple. It is deliberately built at a lower level to emphasise people's humility before God, and it has doors on all four sides, because it is open to everybody.

The Golden Temple is also known as *Harmandir*, the Lord's House. The present building is the fourth Golden Temple on this site and was built in the nineteenth century. The upper part of this beautiful building is covered in gold leaf, and the lower part is marble.

Before taking part in the worship in the gurdwara, a Sikh should bathe. This is not usually a problem in Britain, but in a hot and dusty country like India it usually means that the believer has to bathe in a river or a lake.

Most Sikhs would like to make a pilgrimage to Amritsar and many thousands of pilgrims, Sikhs and non-Sikhs, visit the Golden Temple every day.

FOR DISCUSSION

1 Why do you think Guru Arjan set the Golden Temple in the middle of a lake?

2 Both Hinduism and Sikhism developed in India, yet many features of Sikh building seem to contrast sharply with Hindu ones. List some of the differences. Are these differences between Hindu temples and Sikh gurdwaras also evident in Britain?

◀ *The Golden Temple, Amritsar*

Ganesha, the elephant god, dancing

Siva, the destroyer, riding Nandi, the bull

Things to do — Hindu Temples and Sikh Gurdwaras

1 Find out where your nearest Hindu temple and Sikh gurdwara are, and if possible arrange to visit them. List the main features of the buildings you visit, and sketch the buildings and their features while you are there. (If you can't make a visit, try to do the sketches from the photographs in this book.)

2 Find the names of as many Hindu gods as you can, and what they stand for. Make drawings of these gods and write a brief description of each.

   To start you off, some of the most popular gods are: Krishna; Rama and Sita; Kama, the god of love; Ganesha the elephant; Nandi the bull; Hanuman the monkey; Sarasvati, patron of wisdom; Durga, or Kali, goddess of motherhood; Lakshmi, wife of Vishnu; and, of course, Brahma the creator, Vishnu the preserver, and Siva the destroyer.

3 Make a corner of the classroom into a Hindu shrine. Make a model of one of the gods (perhaps using papier-mâché) and decorate the shrine with flowers, tinsel and lights.

4 Make a list of the ten Gurus of Sikhism, with their dates, and a brief note about each of them.

Guru Nanak and the other nine Gurus

A Quaker Meeting-House at Wooldale, West Yorkshire
Inside the same Meeting-House

25 A Quaker Meeting-House

The Society of Friends, popularly known as Quakers, meet for worship in a simple room or building with no special decorations, furniture or symbols. Where they have special buildings for worship, these are known as Meeting-Houses, not churches. Friends usually sit round in a square or circle, with no special form of service and no minister to lead the worship. They may sit in silence, or one of the group may feel moved to speak a prayer or read aloud, or simply share a thought.

The Society of Friends was founded by George Fox in the seventeenth century. He believed that it was not enough to live your life according to a set of rules; everyone had to think out what he should do for himself, according to the *inner light*, or God within him. The Friends were originally known as Children of Light, until in 1650 George Fox told a judge that he should "Quake and fear at the word of God". The judge called Fox a Quaker, and the name stuck.

It is a long and deep tradition among Friends to search for and work for peace. This is called the *Peace Testimony*. Many Friends are pacifists and refuse to fight, even in time of war. But Quakers have performed many acts of heroism as stretcher bearers and medical orderlies in wartime.

FOR DISCUSSION

1 Why do you think Friends prefer a simple, plain Meeting-House to a church?

2 It must be very difficult for religious persons to know whether their "conscience" really is the "inner light" of God, and not just their own selfish desires. How could a religious person check that the promptings of conscience really were from God? (N.B. There is no easy answer to this question! You might like to ask some religious people you know.)

3 Do you agree with Quaker pacifists that killing people is always wrong and can never be justified even in war? If you did believe that, what would you expect other people to think of you?

A Mormon temple, Birchencliffe, Huddersfield

26 A Mormon Temple

You may have seen a modern church building like this, with the name "Church of Jesus Christ of Latter-Day Saints". But the chances are that few of you have ever been inside one — once such a building, known as a temple, has been dedicated, it is not usually open to the general public.

Despite its name, the Church of Jesus Christ of Latter-Day Saints is not a branch of the Christian church, but a quite separate sect. It owes its origin to Joseph Smith, a farmer's son from New York State, who in the 1820s claimed to have been given some golden plates by an angel from God called Moroni. From these plates, Smith wrote the Book of Mormon, on which Mormonism is based.

Mormons look forward to a time when America, in particular Utah, where Mormonism is now based, will become God's kingdom upon earth. Mormons have always been keen to convert others, and there are now several Mormon temples in Britain. Mormons give one-tenth of their income to the church, and young men have to give up two years to unpaid missionary work. Your home may have been visited by two clean-cut, neatly-dressed missionaries, usually American, carrying a copy of the Book of Mormon.

In the nineteenth century, when they were struggling to survive and expand, Mormons practised polygamy (husbands having more than one wife), but this is now officially discouraged.

FOR DISCUSSION

1 Would you be prepared to give up two years of your life for missionary work, to try to convert others to your beliefs? What do you think makes Mormons so dedicated and committed?

2 All religions expect their members to give money, but not many religious people give as much as one-tenth of their income. Discuss how much you give to charity, or to your religious group if you belong to one. Do you think it is enough? How do you decide how much to give?

A meeting of a House Group. The minister is on the left in the upright chair

27   A House Church

In the early days of Christianity, there were no church buildings — Christians met in the open air, or in ordinary houses. Gradually, as the movement grew and spread, it became necessary for a special building to be set aside for worship, which would be big enough for all the believers in that place and which could be designed for the type of worship which that particular group wished to practise.

Nowadays, many Christians are again experiencing the joy and close fellowship of meeting together in House Groups for worship.

Sometimes, these are members of a Christian church who choose to meet together during the week for prayer, study and worship in the home of one of the group, in addition to their regular worship in church on Sunday.

In other cases, they may be a group of Christians who are dissatisfied with the churches in their neighbourhood and meet together to worship freely in their own way. This may lead to the setting-up of a new denomination — Methodism and the Society of Friends started in this way.

Nowadays, it is generally a group of Fundamentalist or Pentecostalist Christians who set up their own church. Fundamentalists believe that the Bible is the Word of God, and that all their beliefs and actions should be based on what God has spoken in the Bible — hence the name Fundamentalist. Some Fundamentalists, but by no means all, believe that the whole Bible is literally true. Pentecostalists take their name from the events which happened at the Jewish festival of Pentecost soon after the crucifixion of Jesus, when the Spirit of God came upon the disciples and they spoke in strange languages.

FOR DISCUSSION

1   Do you think the more intimate, friendly atmosphere of a House Church could be more helpful than the formal and sometimes cold atmosphere of a big church?

2   Is it possible for a "group within a group", such as a House Group which is part of a church, to meet regularly without becoming a clique? How could such a group avoid the dangers of becoming too inward-looking and exclusive?

3   If some members of a religious group are dissatisfied with the worship or beliefs of the group, should they branch out on their own, or should they stay and work for reform from within?

Things to do — Other Meeting Places

1   Imagine you are a newly-converted Christian, at the time of St. Paul, in the early days of the church. Describe how you meet for worship in the home of one of your friends. (Look up Acts of the Apostles, Chapter 2, verses 42–47; and Chapter 20, verses 7–12.)

2   Imagine you are living in the seventeenth century and you have just heard George Fox preach. You are very moved by what he had to say about "God in everyone" and you want to join him, but you hear that many of his followers have been thrown in jail. Write an account of what happens and what you finally decide to do.

3   Write a newspaper report of a "split" in a local church, which has resulted in a small group of Christians breaking away and forming their own House Church. To make this effective, you will need to include interviews with some of the people concerned: the Minister of the church; the leader of the breakaway group; a friend who sympathises with the leader's views but who decides to stay with the church; and so on.

Religious Festivals

We all celebrate festivals of some kind: *secular* (non-religious), traditional, religious or modern. Sometimes these festivals have very mixed origins. All the great religions of the world mark important events in their calendar with festivals such as the birthday of a leader or founder, thanksgiving for harvest, the ending of a fast, a memorial for a historical event, and so on. The next theme explores some of the major festivals of Christianity, Islam, Judaism, Hinduism, and Sikhism, looking particularly at the ways in which these festivals are celebrated in Britain today.

The choir of Winchester Cathedral singing Christmas carols beside the decorated Christmas tree

A Christmas crib in Exeter Cathedral

28 Christmas

Some of the traditional elements of Christmas can be seen in the top picture — the robed choir in church, singing Christmas carols, and the decorated Christmas tree. The festival of Christmas celebrates the birthday of Jesus Christ — although no one knows the exact date of his birth. It seems likely that Christians in Rome took over the sun-festival of the 25th December from the Roman religion of Mithraism, which was one of the main rivals to Christianity. The story of Jesus has many links with light, e.g. Jesus the Light of the World (John, Chapter 8, verse 12), so this is quite appropriate. Eastern Orthodox Christians celebrate Christmas on the 6th January.

Christmas also seems to have taken over many features of the Roman festival of Saturn, in particular the parties, big meals, and present-giving. Saturnalia used to be held on the 17th December.

Nowadays, Christmas is a time for the family to get together. Presents are exchanged, and a Christmas meal is enjoyed. Great efforts are made to ensure that no one is left out. Most towns and villages have a *crib*, with figures representing Joseph, Mary, the baby Jesus in a manger, donkeys, cattle, the shepherds, and the Wise Men.

The Christmas tree is in fact a pre-Christian symbol. The evergreen was probably a sign of survival through the dark months of winter.

You will find the Christmas story in the New Testament — Matthew, Chapter 1, verses 18–25, and Chapter 2; Luke, Chapters 1 and 2.

FOR DISCUSSION

1 Why do you think the Christians in Rome took over the sun-festival from Mithraism as the date to celebrate the birth of Christ?

2 The giving of presents at Christmas is usually linked with the gifts brought to the infant Jesus by the three Wise Men. Do you think it is a good tradition for children to look forward to presents in this way, or does it encourage people to be selfish and greedy?

3 Where does the story of Father Christmas, or Santa Claus (Saint Nicholas), come from?

Christmas decorations in Regent Street, London

29　Commercial Christmas

Look carefully at the picture of Christmas decorations in Regent Street, London. Do any of the illuminations remind you of traditional Christian Christmas symbols? Christian symbols would be from the Christmas story, such as the three wise men; non-Christian symbols would be such things as holly and mistletoe.

The festival of Christmas, which celebrates the birthday of Jesus Christ, seems nowadays to have become very commercialised — that is, taken over by big business or commerce.

The modern Christmas carol, "Sing High with the Holly", puts it this way:

Where have they hidden you
Child of the manger,
Child of my childhood
And seal of my soul?

They have wrapped me in tinsel
And sold me at counters,
Tuning my song
To the ring of their till.*

The commercial celebration of Christmas seems to start earlier every year. Christmas decorations go up in shop windows and streets, advertisements appear in magazines and newspapers showing "the ideal Christmas present", pre-recorded Christmas music is played continuously in shopping precincts and shops, and we are urged to spend more and more on food, drink and luxuries. It all seems a far cry from that draughty stable two thousand years ago, when Jesus was born.

FOR DISCUSSION

1 Why do you think so many pagan symbols — holly, mistletoe, the yule log, fir trees — have become part of our Christmas celebrations?

2 Do you agree that Christmas has become commercialised? List some examples of this. Do you think anything should — or could — be done to change this?

3 What are the best things about Christmas for you?

*A.J. Lewis; © 1969 Galliard Ltd. From the New Life Hymnbook, published Galliard/Stainer & Bell.

The Olney Pancake Race about to be started

30   Shrove Tuesday

The forty days before Easter are called Lent. This is a period when Christians used to fast — that is, not eat rich foods. The day before Lent is known as *Shrove Tuesday*, because Christians would go to a priest on that day to confess their sins and be *shriven*, which means forgiven. Years ago, people used to put ashes on their heads to show how sorry they were for the things they had done wrong. For this reason, the first day of Lent is known as *Ash Wednesday*.

On Shrove Tuesday, it was the custom to use up all the rich food in the pantry and make pancakes. So another name for Shrove Tuesday is *Pancake Day*.

In Olney, Buckinghamshire, and in various other parts of the country, there is a tradition of having a Pancake Race, where the competitors have to run along carrying a pancake in a frying-pan, tossing the pancake as they go. A visitor from another country would find it very hard to see the connection between this custom and the Christian festival of Easter!

FOR DISCUSSION

1   Can you think of any reasons why the period of fasting before Easter should last forty days?

2   Why did Christians go to confess their sins before the period of Lent?

3   Do you think traditions like the Olney Pancake Race are important, and should be preserved? Are there any traditions like this in the area where you live?

A Good Friday procession re-enacting the Crucifixion, Guatemala

31   Easter

Easter is the major festival of the Christian year. It celebrates the death and *resurrection* (rising to new life) of Jesus Christ. Jesus was put to death on the cross, a cruel form of execution used by the Romans for crimes against the State. His "crime" was that he was said to have claimed to be the King of the Jews. His death is remembered by Christians on Good Friday. Services of remembrance are held in churches. In many parts of the world Christians go on processions of witness through the streets, remembering the time when Jesus carried his cross to the place of execution.

Hot cross buns are eaten on Good Friday. These are rich, spicy buns which symbolise the ending of the fast of Lent, the period before Easter.

But Good Friday is not the end of the story. Christians believe that two days later, on the first Easter Sunday, Jesus rose from the dead. This is celebrated by joyful services in church, with hymns such as

Jesus Christ is risen today, Alleluia!

Our triumphant holy day, Alleluia!

On Easter Sunday in an Eastern Orthodox church, the priest proclaims: "Christ is Risen!" and the people respond: "He is risen indeed!"

In most Christian churches in Britain, the date of Easter is calculated in the same way as the Jewish Passover. Jesus was a Jew, and the crucifixion took place at the time of the Passover festival. The Last Supper which Jesus had with his disciples (see Matthew, Chapter 26, verses 17 – 30) was most probably a Passover Seder meal. The custom of giving Easter eggs as a symbol of new life is probably taken from the Jewish Seder meal.

You will find the Easter story in the New Testament (Matthew, Chapters 26 – 28, or Luke, Chapters 22 – 24).

FOR DISCUSSION

1   Why is Easter the major festival of the Christian year?

2   Whatever actually happened on that first Easter Sunday, something changed the disciples from a rabble of frightened men, hiding in fear of their lives, into a fearless band, prepared to preach their faith publicly and, if necessary, to die for it. What do you think happened?

Two views of a Whit Walk at Saddleworth, Greater Manchester

32　Whitsun

Seven weeks after Passover, the disciples were together to celebrate the festival of Shavuot, or Pentecost, when they had a wonderful experience, which they described as being "filled with the Spirit of God". It seemed to them to be a fulfilment of the prophecy of Joel:

"The day shall come when I will pour out my spirit on all mankind." (Joel, Chapter 2, verse 28.)

You can read the story of what happened to the disciples at Pentecost in the New Testament — Acts of the Apostles, Chapter 2, verses 1–4.

Pentecost became known as the birthday of the Christian church, and it was a popular day of the year for baptisms. In Britain, people being baptised at Pentecost wore white clothes, and Pentecost came to be known as White Sunday, or Whitsun.

In parts of Lancashire and Yorkshire, it is a tradition for Christians to go on walks of witness at Whitsun, known as the Whit Walks. Usually, the members of each church or Sunday School meet at their own place of worship and have a short service, after which they walk in procession through the streets of their town or village. They stop at certain places and sing, sometimes meeting up with the members of other churches.

FOR DISCUSSION

1　Why was Pentecost known as the birthday of the church?

2　Why did people wear white for baptisms?

3　What do you think is the purpose of the Whit Walks in the North of England?

"Christ driving the traders from the Temple" by El Greco

Things to do — Christian Festivals

1 Make a Christmas Crib — either a traditional one, with a stable, shepherds and wise men, or a modern one, imagining Jesus being born today, perhaps in a garage or a railway station.

2 Write a Christmas story about a lonely old person with nothing to look forward to except a Christmas alone. Suddenly the doorbell rings. . . .

3 Some of the greatest paintings of Western civilisation have been inspired by events in the life of Jesus. Try your hand at painting the Christmas scene, or the Crucifixion.

4 Design some Christmas cards which carry the real message of Christmas in a way that non-religious, non-churchgoing people will understand.

5 Improvise a Pentecost play, based on the gift of the Holy Spirit to the apostles. Remember that onlookers thought the apostles were all mad, or drunk, until Peter gave his speech explaining what had happened. (Acts of the Apostles, Chapter 2, verses 14–41.)

6 Write an account of the first Christian Pentecost, as if you had been a scribe listening to Peter's speech.

7 Imagine you are living at an earlier time — say, the eighteenth century — and you have been baptised into the church on Whit Sunday. Write a letter to a friend, describing the ceremony and what you experienced.

You should read about everyday life at that time in reference books in the library, to get background details, and you could perhaps talk to someone who has been baptised or confirmed recently, to find out what the service was like and what it felt like to take part.

Men at the breaking of fast prayers overflowing a mosque at Kano

A mullah, or holy man,
about to start reading
the Qur'an in a mosque

33 Ramadan

The Muslim year is based on lunar months. The ninth month of the Muslim year is called *Ramadan* and is observed as a complete month of fasting. From dawn to dusk, all adult Muslims abstain completely from food and drink. This is observed very strictly, as it is one of the Five Pillars of Faith, found in the Qur'an. The only concessions are for the sick, for pregnant women, and for travellers, who are allowed to make up the days of fasting at a later date. During the month, Muslims are even stricter than usual in their religious observance; for example, many men go to the mosque every evening to say their prayers together.

As well as fasting, Ramadan is a month of rejoicing at the handing-down of the Qur'an. One night in the month, called the *Night of Power*, is the anniversary of the first revelation by the Angel Gabriel to Muhammad. The rest of the month is devoted to the reading of the Qur'an.

Before the fast ends, Muslims have to give to charity, to ensure that everyone, even the poor, will be able to afford to buy food. This is called *Zakat-ul-Fitr*, the charity of fast-breaking.

FOR DISCUSSION

1   What is the longest you have ever gone without food? Could you go without food every day between dawn and dusk, for a month? Muslims say that the purpose of fasting is to teach self-discipline, and to remind people what it is like to be poor. Do you think this is a worthwhile thing to attempt?

2   How difficult would it be to obey the fasting rule in Britain, if you were at work all day?

3   Do you know of festivals in other religions which involve fasting? Are these strictly observed?

Muslims going to the Eid-ul-Fitr salat at Fatehpur Sikri, India

A selection of Eid cards

34 Eid-ul-Fitr

When the new moon is sighted, signifying the end of Ramadan and the beginning of the month of *Shawal*, Muslim children become very excited. The first of Shawal is the festival of *Eid-ul-Fitr*, the breaking of the fast. All the family get up early, and if possible they take a bath or shower so that everyone is clean for the visit to the mosque. Most Muslims stay away from work, and the children do not go to school. There is a special salat in the mosque during the morning. If there are two or three mosques in that village or town, only one will be used for this special service, so that as many Muslims as possible are gathered together. Many people wear new clothes, and there is a general air of festivity.

After the mosque service, everyone goes home, often to big family gatherings. The houses are decorated with Eid greetings cards, and presents are exchanged. Then the family sits down to a special Eid meal, the first midday meal for a month.

The Eid party may go on for most of the day, but many Muslims also have a tradition on this day of visiting the graves of relatives, and saying prayers.

FOR DISCUSSION

1 Make a list of the ways in which Eid-ul-Fitr is similar to Christmas, and a list of the differences.

2 Why do you think Muslims take a shower and wear new clothes for Eid?

3 Why is Eid especially exciting for children?

35   Eid-ul-Adha

Another of the Five Pillars of Islam is *Hajj*, pilgrimage. Every Muslim is expected to make the pilgrimage to Mecca, in Saudi Arabia, unless he is sick or too poor to make the journey. The photograph shows the great mosque at Mecca, during *Dhul-Hijja*, the month of pilgrimage. In the centre of the picture is the Ka'aba, the small building which the Qur'an says was built by Abraham and his son Ishmael. There is a black stone in one wall of the Ka'aba which every pilgrim must touch or kiss during the pilgrimage.

The climax of the pilgrimage events takes place at Mina, a village outside Mecca, the traditional site where Muslims believe the Devil tempted Abraham to sacrifice Ishmael. A sheep or a goat is sacrificed by the pilgrims in remembrance that Abraham sacrificed a ram instead of his son. The same sacrifice is made on the tenth day of Dhul-Hijja by Muslims all over the world, not just those on the pilgrimage. The sacrifice of a sheep or goat symbolises the devotion of the believer to God in total obedience. Traditionally, one-third of the slaughtered animal is given to the poor.

The sacrifice is followed by prayers in the mosque, after which the worshippers wish each other *"Eid Mubarak"* — happy festival.

This festival is called *Eid-ul-Adha*, which means feast of sacrifice. It is known as the "major" festival, although it is not celebrated with as many activities as Eid-ul-Fitr, the "minor" festival.

FOR DISCUSSION

1   How difficult would it be for a Muslim living in Britain to go on the Hajj?

2   Why do you think Eid-ul-Fitr, the minor Eid, has become in many ways a "bigger" festival than Eid-ul-Adha?

3   In Britain, the slaughter of animals for food is governed by official regulations, but an animal offered for the Muslim festival of Eid-ul-Adha has to have its throat cut in the manner laid down by Islamic law. Do you foresee any difficulties or conflict here?

◀ *Crowds of Muslim pilgrims around the Ka'aba in the courtyard of the Great Mosque at Mecca*

A rabbi blowing a shofar at Rosh Hashanah

36 Rosh Hashanah and Yom Kippur

Rosh Hashanah is the Jewish New Year's Day, which falls in the Jewish seventh month, *Tishri* (September or October). In accordance with the Torah, this is a day of rest, proclaimed by the blowing of a *shofar*, or ram's horn. (See Leviticus, Chapter 23, verses 24–25.)

At Rosh Hashanah, Jewish people wish each other well for the coming year. There is a tradition of eating a slice of apple dipped in honey, and saying: "May it be the Lord's will to renew us for a year which will be good and sweet."

The ten days from Rosh Hashanah are the days of repentance, during which Jews try to put right any wrong they have done. The tenth day of the month is *Yom Kippur*, the Day of Atonement, a special day set aside for people to *repent*, that is, to be truly sorry for everything they have done wrong. Jews believe that if they truly repent, God will forgive them their sins. To mark Yom Kippur, adult Jews go without food and drink for twenty-five hours.

An Israeli soldier wearing a prayer shawl at his morning prayers near his armoured car whilst on duty in Syria

Since the State of Israel was proclaimed in 1948, there have been a number of conflicts between Israel and the surrounding Arab States. One of these, in 1973, began on the Day of Atonement, and is known as the Yom Kippur war.

FOR DISCUSSION

1 Most Jews and Christians believe that if you are really sorry for things you have done wrong, God will forgive you. Is it enough merely to *be* sorry, or should you try to make amends for things you have done wrong? Why do you think the Jews believe it is important to have a special time for repentance?

2 How does the Jewish belief about repentance and forgiveness compare with that of other religions, e.g. Christianity?

3 The struggle of the Jewish people to regain their ancient homeland of Israel is a very moving story. But the setting-up of the state of Israel has involved the displacement of many Palestinian Arabs, as the Yom Kippur war reminds us. Where do your sympathies lie? Have events such as the Israeli involvement in Lebanon affected your point of view?

A booth in a London synagogue at Succoth

37 Succoth

The Jewish festival of Succoth falls five days after Yom Kippur. It is a traditional celebration of the fruit harvest and lasts seven days. *Sukkot* in Hebrew means a hut or booth. A booth is a rough shelter made from the branches of trees. The festival is sometimes called Tabernacles in English, from the old English word meaning booth or shelter.

The booths are a reminder of the time when the Israelites, led by Moses, wandered through the wilderness searching for the Promised Land. In hot countries the booths are built in the open and Jewish families sleep out in them. In cooler countries, such as Britain, booths are usually built indoors, and some of the best examples are to be found in synagogues, like the one in the photograph. Fruit of all kinds, especially oranges, lemons and grapefruit, are hung inside the booth as a sign of God's love for his people in providing food for them.

During the festival of Succoth, joyful celebrations are held in the synagogues. The boys and men hold long palm branches, called *lulav*, in the right hand, and a yellow citrus fruit rather like a lemon, called *etrog*, in the left hand. This is to fulfil God's commandment in the Torah:

"Take the fruit of citrus trees, palm fronds, leafy branches, and willows from the riverside, and rejoice before the Lord your God for seven days." (Leviticus, Chapter 23, verse 40.)

A rabbi holding lulav and etrog

FOR DISCUSSION

1 Do you think it is a good idea to keep alive aspects of a people's history by symbolic actions such as the building of booths?

2 Can you think of any events in British or American history which are kept alive in this way?

A nine-branched menorah alight in a Jewish home

38   Hanukah and Purim

About 165 B.C.E., the Greek ruler of Syria, Antiochus, ordered the Jews to give up their traditional ways of worship. He had a statue of himself put up in the Temple in Jerusalem, destroyed the Torah scrolls, and — worst of all — sacrificed a pig on the altar. Judah Maccabee (the Hammerer) led a revolt against Antiochus. After three years of fighting, Judah regained control of Jerusalem and cleansed the Temple. The everlasting light was relit, but there was only enough oil for one night. Miraculously, this oil lasted for eight nights, until fresh supplies arrived.

This miracle is remembered every year in the Jewish festival of *Hanukah*, which means Dedication and takes place in December.

A nine-branched candleholder or *menorah* is lit in Jewish homes during this festival. The first candle is called the servant candle, or *shamach*. On the first night of the festival, one candle is lit from the shamach, on the second night two candles are lit, and so on through the eight nights of the festival. (This nine-branched menorah is not to be confused with the seven-branched menorah which has become a symbol of Judaism, and is often used in the decoration of synagogues.)

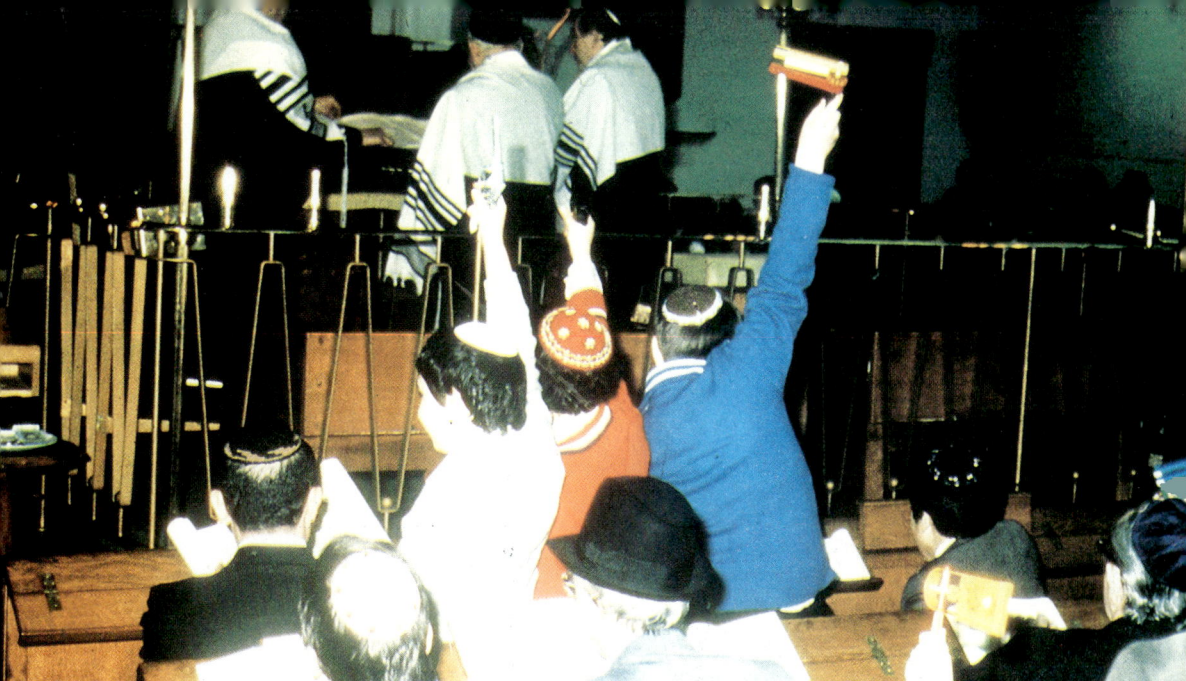

Boys waving rattles and firing cap-guns in a synagogue at Purim

Another Jewish festival based on a story about persecution of the Jewish people is *Purim*, which takes place in March. This is taken from the story of Esther (see the Book of Esther, in the Hebrew Bible — the Old Testament). Purim means "lots" or dice, and the festival is so called because Haman, chief minister to the Persian king, cast lots to decide the date on which all the Jews in the Persian empire should be killed. His evil scheme was thwarted thanks to the courage of Queen Esther. When the story of Esther is told at this festival, Jewish children wave a rattle, boo and hiss, just like at a pantomime, whenever Haman's name is mentioned.

FOR DISCUSSION

1   Can you think of any British heroes who, like Judah Maccabee, fought bravely against invaders? Are there any stories about these heroes? Are there any other stories like the one of the miraculous oil in the Temple? Do you think these stories are true, or could they have been exaggerated in the telling?

2   The Jewish people have suffered terribly from persecutions over the centuries, culminating in the horrors of the Holocaust, when six million Jews died at the hands of the Nazis. What do you think is the main reason for prejudice against Jews? What can be done to prevent it happening again?

A Jewish family at table for the Passover Seder meal

39   Pesach and Shavuot

Pesach (Passover) is the Jewish festival which celebrates the exodus from Egypt of the Israelites. The name Passover comes from the Biblical story of the plague in which the first-born of every Egyptian household was killed, but the angel of God passed over the Israelite houses and their first-born were not killed. (See Exodus, Chapters 1–15.)

On Passover Eve, the men go to the synagogue, then return home for a special meal, the *Seder*. Seder means order, and there is a special order of service, written in a book called the *Haggadah* (telling), which tells the story of Passover. The meal starts with the blessing of the wine; four glasses of wine are drunk during the meal, as a reminder of God's four promises to Moses (Exodus, Chapter 6, verses 6, 7).

The meal itself has a number of symbolic items: parsley in salt water (the bitterness of slavery); three pieces of unleavened bread, or *matzoth* (the hurried departure, when the Israelites had no time to leaven the dough); a baked or roasted egg (representing the hope of new life); a roasted shank bone of lamb (the lamb which was sacrificed); and a mixture of apples, nuts, cinnamon and wine, called *haroset* (the mortar used by the Hebrew slaves in Egypt).

The youngest boy asks "Why is this night different from all other nights?" The child then asks four questions about the Passover, the answers to which tell the story of the night when the Israelites escaped from Egypt. A fifth cup of wine is traditionally left untouched for the prophet Elijah, whose return would mean the coming of the Messiah.

Another major Jewish festival is *Shavuot*. This means Weeks, and is so called because it comes exactly seven weeks after Pesach. It is a summer festival celebrating the corn harvest, when the synagogue is decorated with flowers and plants, and the Book of Ruth (from the Torah, or Christian Old Testament) is read. Shavuot also celebrates the giving of the Law. It is also known as Pentecost, from the Greek for "fiftieth" (day).

FOR DISCUSSION

1 Why is Passover so important to the Jews?
2 Do you think the Jewish Seder meal is a good way of teaching children about an important event in Jewish history?

Things to do — Muslim and Jewish Festivals

1 The Muslim calendar is based on lunar months, and began in 622 C.E. (Common Era), the year of the Hijra, when the Prophet Muhammad left Mecca to go to Medina. So 622 C.E. = 0 A.H. (A.H. = After the Hijra).

   To calculate the date according to the Muslim calendar, use the formula:

$$\text{A.H.} = \frac{33}{32} \times (\text{C.E.} -622)$$

So the year 1902 C.E., for example, would be, according to the Muslim calendar,

$$\frac{33}{32} \times (1902-622)$$

$$= \frac{33}{32} \times 1280$$

$$= 1320 \text{ A.H.}$$

Calculate the following dates according to the Muslim calendar:

   1984 C.E.

   1990 C.E.

   2000 C.E.

2 Because of the lunar calendar, Muslim festivals occur about eleven days earlier each year. The first day of Ramadan in 1983 was the 12th June. Calculate when it will fall, approximately, in 1984, 1985, 1986, 1987, 1988, 1989 and 1990. Remember that the exact date depends upon the sighting of the New Moon.

3 Design an Eid card for Eid-ul-Fitr, the breaking of the fast.

4 Imagine you are a Muslim living in Britain and you have received a generous present for Eid from your grandparents, who live in Bangladesh. Write them a letter, thanking them for the present and describing how you celebrated Ramadan and Eid-ul-Fitr in this country.

5 Fasting is very important to a Muslim. Write an essay explaining why it is so important to Muslims to fast during Ramadan, and comparing the Muslim practice of fasting during daylight hours for a whole month with the Christian observance of fasting during Lent and the Jewish fast of Yom Kippur.

6　Listen carefully to the television news every night for a week, or read the International News page of a newspaper every day. Count the number of times the State of Israel is referred to, and list the incidents described and the other countries involved. Write a newspaper article yourself, summing up the rights and wrongs of the matters under review.

7　If you have a special room for R.E. it may be possible for your class to build a tabernacle or booth in the classroom. You may not be able to get palm and myrtle branches, but try to get something similar such as willow. Then imagine you were with Moses, wandering in the wilderness. Describe your feelings of relief when at last you reached the Promised Land, and could build a permanent home.

8　Make a nine-branched menorah, with candleholders instead of oil lamps. Write a letter to a friend, as if you had been with Judah Maccabee when he re-took the Temple, describing the miracle of the oil. With the help of the Music department, learn the song "Hanukah"* and prepare a Hanukah assembly, using your letter, your menorah, and the song.

9　Read the story of Esther, and make it into a short play, with improvised dialogue.

10　With the co-operation of the Home Economics department, make as many as possible of the ingredients of a Seder meal. Then act out the Seder meal in an assembly, telling the story of the Passover in your own words and allowing as many people as possible to taste the food.

*The song "Hanukah" is to be found in "Harlequin — 44 songs round the year", published A. & C. Black Ltd.

A huge statue of Ravana ready for burning

40 Dussehra

Hinduism is rich in festivals, just as it is rich in gods. This huge statue of Ravana was built for the festival of *Dussehra*. 'Das' or 'Dus' means ten, and Dussehra is celebrated on the tenth day of a longer festival called *Navaratri*.

Navaratri is a festival devoted to the goddess Durga, symbol of motherhood. At Navaratri, the great story of Rama and Sita is told. This is contained in a famous Indian epic called the Ramayana. In this story, Rama's wife Sita is stolen from him by a demon called Ravana, and Rama manages to win her back with the help of the goddess Durga.

Ravana being burnt

A huge statue of Ravana is burnt as part of a great fireworks display, symbolising good triumphing over evil. Dussehra is a time to celebrate friendship and loyalty, and during this time Hindus try to heal any quarrels or conflicts that have taken place during the previous year.

FOR DISCUSSION

1 Compare Dussehra with other festivals you know of which contain similar elements — good triumphing over evil, the burning of an effigy, making up quarrels. What are the similarities and differences?

2 Epic stories — ancient tales of heroes and giants, warriors and demons, good versus evil — are found in all traditions. Can you think of any English epics or legends which compare with the story of Rama and Sita? What are the similarities? Why do you think these tales were told — for pure entertainment or for some deeper reason?

41 Divali

Divali is really a continuation of the festivals of Navaratri and Dussehra. The word *Divali* means "a row of lights", and at this time, homes and other buildings are decorated with many lights along windows, doorsteps and balconies.

There are two traditions which are celebrated at Divali. One is the triumphant return of Rama to his Kingdom with his wife Sita, the climax of the Ramayana story. Another is that the goddess Lakshmi, wife of Vishnu the preserver, visits homes which are decorated with lights, bringing gifts and good luck. This is celebrated in the home by making an offering of fire before an image of Lakshmi.

An offering being made to Lakshmi in a Hindu home at Divali

Divali is a joyful festival with presents for the children and the sending of Divali cards, and family parties.

FOR DISCUSSION

1 Can you think of any other festivals which are festivals of light? How do they compare with Divali?

2 Does the visit of Lakshmi with gifts remind you of any other festival? What are the similarities and differences?

◀ Divali lights being lit

Coloured powders being sold at Holi

Brightly-coloured powder being thrown at Holi

42　Holi

Holi is an outdoor festival to celebrate the coming of spring, although as it falls in February, it usually seems a bit early in Britain! It is a noisy, jolly, messy festival, when coloured powders are sold to be mixed with water and squirted over all and sundry. Children love it, of course. In Hindu villages, bonfires are lit and mothers carry their children round the fire to ask Agni, god of fire, to bless them.

There is a story from Hindu mythology which goes with the festival of Holi. It is the story of an Indian king who declared that his people should stop worshipping the gods, and should worship him instead. This king had a son, Prahlada, who was very religious. So devoted was Prahlada to the gods that he even learnt his alphabet with the aid of the names of the gods: A for Agni, B for Brahma, K for Krishna, and so on. Prahlada refused to obey his father, and the king was so enraged that he asked his daughter, Holika, to get rid of the boy.

Holika had the magical power of being able to walk unharmed through fire. She picked up Prahlada and, carrying him in her arms, stepped into a fire. Unfortunately for Holika, what she did not know was that her magic worked only when she walked through fire alone. She was burnt up, and Prahlada, who had been quietly chanting the names of the gods, came out of the fire unharmed.

FOR DISCUSSION

1 Spring festivals, which celebrate the passing of winter, are found in every culture. In Britain, the name of the Saxon goddess of spring, Eostre, is preserved in the Christian festival of Easter. Why do you think springtime was so important to people who depended on the land for their livelihood?

2 Can you think of any other festivals or customs which involve playing tricks on people? Have you ever taken part in such tricks? What did you do?

Krishna as the charioteer of Prince Arjuna

Krishna with Prince Arjuna

43   The Birthday of Krishna

Krishna is one form of the god Vishnu. In the great epic poem called the *Mahabharata* (maha = great, Bharat = India), Krishna appears as the charioteer of Prince Arjuna in a great battle. The section of the poem describing the battle, in which Krishna teaches Arjuna about the problems of life, is called the *Bhagavad Gita*, the song of the adorable one. This has been described as the high point of the Hindu religion.

The birthday of Krishna is celebrated by waiting up until midnight — the time Krishna is supposed to have been born — and then singing and dancing to welcome the new-born child. Many people go to the temple to wait for midnight, and the celebrations often go on all night. Sweet foods are shared out, and stories about Krishna are told.

There are also many popular stories about Krishna, particularly about the naughty tricks he got up to when he was a child. The word 'Krishna' means black, and Krishna is often portrayed as dark or blue-skinned, as in both of these illustrations.

FOR DISCUSSION

1 How does the Hindu festival celebrating the birth of Krishna compare with the ways in which Christians celebrate the birth of Jesus?

2 Can you think of other religions in which a god 'descends' to earth and takes human form? Why is this theme so central to religion?

A Sikh family in the Punjab at Baisakhi

44   Baisakhi

This photograph shows a Sikh family in the Punjab, north India, at *Baisakhi*, the first month of the New Year in the Sikh calendar.

On the first day of the month of Baisakhi in 1699, the tenth Guru of the Sikhs, Gobind Singh, called all his followers to a special gathering. He appeared before them carrying a sword, and asked for a volunteer who was prepared to die for his Guru and faith. When one man volunteered, Guru Gobind Singh took him into a tent. There was a swish and a thud, and Guru Gobind Singh came out with his sword dripping with blood. This happened with four more volunteers. Then Guru Gobind Singh brought the five men out, wearing new turbans and uniforms. Was it a miracle, or just Guru Gobind Singh's way of showing his followers that they had to be prepared to die for their faith?

Next, Guru Gobind Singh mixed a nectar of sugar and water, sprinkled it on his five volunteers, and gave them some to drink from the same bowl. Then he asked them to do the same for him. This was the formation of the *Khalsa*, or brotherhood of Pure Ones. Every male Sikh who is baptised into the Khalsa in this way takes the name *Singh* (lion) and every female the name *Kaur* (princess).

Since 1699, Baisakhi has become for the Sikhs a celebration of the birthday of the Khalsa brotherhood.

The Sikhs became famous for their courage in battle, particularly in their struggle for religious freedom under the Mughal (Muslim) rulers of India. The picture below is called 'The Forty Saved Ones'. The Forty Saved Ones were the martyrs of the Battle of Muktsar, who originally chose to abandon the Guru in order to save their lives, but before doing so they had to sign a Deed of Renouncement. A group of forty Sikhs who did so, however, relented, rejoined the Guru, fought bravely and died as martyrs. Here, their dying leader, Mohan Singh of Rataul, requests the Guru to pardon them and tear up the statement they had signed.

Guru Gobind Singh with the dying Mohan Singh

FOR DISCUSSION

1 What do you think happened on that Baisakhi day in 1699?

2 Do you think it is significant that Guru Gobind Singh asked his followers to baptise him, too? What do you think it meant? Can you think of any parallels in other religions?

3 Do you know of other instances where followers or believers have had their faith put to the test?

Sobha Singh

45 The Birthday of Guru Nanak

Guru Nanak was born into a Hindu family in the fifteenth century C.E. He had a deep religious experience which led him to become a religious teacher. He and the succeeding Gurus taught that there was only one God and that everyone is equal before God. The word Sikh means learner or disciple.

Any holy day associated with the birth or death of a Sikh Guru is called a Gurpurb. Sikhs today have a special Gurpurb to celebrate the birth of Guru Nanak. In India, this is celebrated by an open-air procession carrying the Sikh holy scripture, the Guru Granth Sahib, on a float. In Britain, outdoor processions are not always practical, but every Gurpurb is celebrated by a continuous reading of the whole of the Guru Granth Sahib, called an *Akhand Path*. This takes about forty-eight hours and is read in relays.

The Akhand Path is timed so that the final reading takes place during the Sunday worship in the Gurdwara, after which a talk is given, based on the life and death of Guru Nanak, and hymns are sung. Then everybody stays behind for a meal together, called the *Guru Ka Langar*.

A granthi reading the Guru Granth Sahib in the Golden Temple, Amritsar

FOR DISCUSSION

1   Why do Sikhs celebrate the birthday of Guru Nanak? Can you see any similarities between the way Sikhs celebrate Guru Nanak's birthday, and the way Christians celebrate Christmas?

2   Why do you think the whole of the Guru Granth Sahib is read at a Gurpurb?

3   What do you think is the significance of the Guru Ka Langar? Are there any other festivals where a meal is an important part of the celebrations?

Things to do — Hindu and Sikh Festivals

1 Make some Divali cards, using the symbol of light and scenes from the story of Rama and Sita.

2 Imagine you have been on a visit to India, during the spring festival of Holi. Write a letter home, describing what happened.

3 Make up your own 'epic story' (perhaps not as long as the Mahabharata!) about a god who becomes a man and goes about on earth.

Krishna and the Gopis (milkmaids)

4 Write an account of what happened on the first of Baisakhi, 1699, as if you were an observer who was present. Don't forget to include the reactions of the crowd when Guru Gobind Singh said he wanted the head of a Sikh.

  You might be able to get together in groups to prepare a dramatised version of the formation of the Khalsa.

5 Most Sikh Gurdwaras, and many books about Sikhism, contain pictures of the ten Gurus. Copy one of these pictures to give you some idea of the style, then draw a picture of Guru Nanak or one of the other Gurus from your imagination.

◀ *Guru Gobind Singh, the tenth Guru of the Sikhs*

Well-dressing at Hope, Derbyshire

Beating the bounds at the Tower of London

46 Ancient Customs

Many old customs can be traced back to primitive times, when people were very dependent on Nature and its moods — their lives were seriously affected by storm, drought, flood and famine. Water is obviously necessary for survival, and in several villages in England the old wells are dressed at Ascensiontide with flowers and berries. Ascensiontide is the time when Christians celebrate the return of Jesus to Heaven. Ascension Day is the Thursday of the week beginning four weeks after Easter Sunday. In some Derbyshire villages, the well-dressings depict Biblical scenes. This one, at the village of Hope, shows the Egyptian Princess finding the infant Moses in the bulrushes.

The custom of well-dressing goes back at least as far as the time of the Black Death in the fourteenth century. Several villages in Derbyshire escaped the plague because of the purity of their water supply.

Many Christian festivals took over from pagan festivals — Easter, for example. Other festivals and customs may have an agricultural origin — such as the tradition of "beating the bounds". The parish clergyman used to walk round the boundaries of his parish once a year, on Rogation Day, followed by the choirboys or schoolboys, who every so often would "beat" the boundaries with willow canes. The priest would ask for blessings on the crops, and this explains the name of the festival — rogation is from the Latin word for "ask". This ceremony is still carried out every three years at the Tower of London with Beefeaters (Yeomen of the Guard) and choirboys taking part.

FOR DISCUSSION

1 Do you think that ancient traditions such as these should be preserved? What are the arguments for and against?

2 Do you think that modern man has lost something important by living in cities and losing touch with Nature? If so, how could this be rediscovered?

New Year celebrations in Trafalgar Square, London

47 New Year Celebrations

With Christmas and New Year being so close, it always used to be the custom to take a long holiday which covered both — the Twelve Days of Christmas. It was only during the Industrial Revolution, with the factory owners needing to get maximum production from their factories and mills, that people started to go back to work between Christmas and New Year. Nowadays, it is again becoming more common for people to take a holiday from Christmas Eve until the 2nd or 3rd January.

New Year in Scotland — Hogmanay — has always been a time of great celebration, and New Year's Eve parties, when people stay up to see in the New Year, are common everywhere.

One very old custom, which goes back to pre-Christian times, is the lighting of New Year fires, and this is still carried on in some parts of Scotland and the North of England. In Allendale, Northumberland, barrels of burning tar are carried in procession to light a New Year's fire at midnight.

Another old custom, still followed in Scotland and in the North of England, is *first-footing*. As midnight strikes, there is a knock on the door, and a neighbour comes in bringing a piece of coal for the fire — the first person to cross the threshold in the New Year. It used to be thought that this would bring good luck and prosperity for the year — especially if the "first-footer" was a tall, dark stranger!

In London, in Trafalgar Square, many thousands of people gather to celebrate New Year. In 1982/83, this led to a double tragedy when two people were trampled to death by the crowds. There was subsequently a call for such street gatherings to be banned, or at least much better controlled.

FOR DISCUSSION

1 Why do people celebrate the New Year? How do you celebrate the New Year in your family?

2 What other New Year customs do you know about?

3 Do you think street gatherings, such as the New Year's Eve celebrations in Trafalgar Square, should be banned? If not, how should they be controlled so that accidents do not happen?

48   The Chinese New Year

The Chinese New Year is calculated by the lunar calendar. According to an ancient tradition, the kitchen gods go off to report on the state of the household kitchen before New Year, so a week before the festival the kitchen is thoroughly cleaned. On New Year's Eve, the kitchen gods are welcomed back with firecrackers.

New Year itself for the Chinese is a time of family reunions, with parties, presents and special foods. Children are given "lucky money" in red envelopes, and the houses are filled with flowers and lanterns.

New Year celebrations in Chinatown, San Francisco

To keep away evil spirits a marvellous multi-coloured dragon or lion dances through the streets which are often decorated with flags, banners and lanterns. The dragons in the photographs are made up by two men, but sometimes they can be individual ones and sometimes they can be made up by half a dozen or more.

FOR DISCUSSION

1   How does the Chinese New Year compare with Christmas? What are the religious elements in the Chinese New Year celebrations?

2   What do you think is the origin of the Dragon?

3   Do you think that customs from other countries, such as the Dragon Dance, will survive in Britain? Can you think of any other ancient traditions which originally came from other lands and which are now firmly part of this country's tradition?

◀ *A Chinese dragon in a British street*

A flower festival at Lavenham Church, Suffolk

A float in the flower parade at Spalding, Lincolnshire

49 A Flower Festival

The top photograph shows the church at Lavenham in Suffolk decorated for a flower festival. Such festivals are wonderfully artistic, with flower arrangements representing all kinds of Biblical, historical or local scenes.

The idea of arranging flowers at a temple or place of worship, as an offering to a god, is a very old one. The Romans used to have a flower festival called Floralia in honour of Flora, their goddess of flowers. The Chinese have an ancient flower festival, when the women and children wear elaborate head-dresses made out of flowers. But above all, we get most of our ideas about flower-arranging from the Japanese art of *ikebana*, which means "living flowers". The Japanese have many flower festivals, which probably date back to the offering of flowers to Buddha, the Enlightened One, whose followers went to Japan from India in the sixth century C.E.

Some flower festivals today have completely lost their religious origin and are purely secular festivals. One such is the Flower Parade at Spalding in Lincolnshire, where thousands and thousands of tulip heads, by-products of the bulb-growing industry, are arranged in intricate patterns on steel frames on tractors.

FOR DISCUSSION

1 Think of some special occasions when people are given flowers. Where, in your home, would a special arrangement of flowers be placed? Who would do the arranging? Is it usually a woman's job? If so, why do you think this is?

2 "Say it with flowers." How can flowers express a message? Think of some flowers which express feelings, such as love, sympathy, etc. Why do you think these flowers have come to have these meanings?

3 Why do you think flower festivals are so popular? Is it just the beauty and colour of the arrangements? Or does a flower festival strike a deep-seated, religious chord?

Two girls helping with Harvest Festival preparations at Lower Peover Church, Cheshire

50   A Harvest Festival

Harvest Festivals in Christian churches are still very popular, especially in rural areas. The photograph shows the church in the village of Lower Peover, Cheshire, decorated for the Harvest Festival. Offerings of fruit, vegetables and flowers are brought to the church and arranged beautifully as an offering of thanks to God for the harvest. Traditional harvest hymns, sung at this time, echo the theme of gratitude to God:

Come, ye thankful people, come,
Raise the song of harvest home.
All is safely gathered in
Ere the winter storms begin.

Harvest time has always been a time of rejoicing for country people. Years ago, in the days before machines, nearly all the villagers would have been hard at work in the fields for weeks with their scythes, cutting and stacking the corn. After the sheaves had dried, they would have been pitch-forked on to the wagons and taken to the farm, the last wagon being decorated with ribbons and flowers. The farmer and his wife would give a grand supper in the farmhouse or in a barn for all the workers who had helped bring the harvest home.

The last few pieces of corn harvested would be twisted and plaited into the shape of a cross or a person. This was called a *corn dolly*. It represented the spirit of the corn, and was kept safe over the winter to be planted with the new seed next spring.

Corn dollies — a cross and a "maiden"

FOR DISCUSSION

1 If we thank God for a successful harvest, do we also blame God if the crops fail?

2 Why do you think the corn dolly was planted the following spring?

3 Can you see any similarities between the Christian Harvest Festival and the Jewish festivals of Succoth and Shavuot?

4 Nowadays, the Harvest Festival is often seen as an opportunity for the well-fed Western nations to remember that two-thirds of the world are starving. What, in your opinion, could be done to solve the problem?

Things to do — Festivals

1   Think of a festival or special occasion in your neighbourhood which is celebrated with a procession of some kind — perhaps a summer carnival. List the different things in the festival procession - bands, floats, fancy dress, etc. Choose one of these and make a large drawing of it. If your classroom has a pinboard for display, the drawings could be pinned up like a procession.

2   Make a list of festivals — religious or otherwise — which your family celebrates every year (e.g. Christmas, birthdays, New Year). Describe briefly how you celebrate each of these festivals.

3   Write a story about a festival. A young boy or girl is taken to a festival in a big town, and gets separated from his/her parents. The organisers of the festival mistake the child for someone who is supposed to be playing a leading part in the festival, and dress the child up in the special costume. . . .

4   Ask your grandparents, or any elderly people you know, whether they remember any old customs or festivals which have now died out. If they do remember any, ask them to tell you all about how it used to be celebrated. You may be able to borrow a cassette recorder to record what they tell you, so that you can write it out for the class.

For Further Reading

Christian Churches

The Story of our Churches and Cathedrals: *R. Bowood.* Ladybird
   Books.
Visiting a Community Church: *G. Palmer.* Lutterworth.
The Pentecostal Churches: *K. Ottoson.* Wheaton.
What to look for outside a church: *P.J. Hunt.* Ladybird.
We discover the Church: *R. Fice and M. Simkiss.* E.J. Arnold.
Churches: *H. Pluckrose.* Mills & Boon.
What to look for inside a church: *P.J. Hunt.* Ladybird.
The Christian Faith and its Symbols: *J. Thompson.* Edward Arnold.
Visiting an Anglican Church: *S.E. Tompkins.* Lutterworth.
A Pictorial History of English Architecture: *J. Betjeman.* Murray.
Thinking about Christianity: *R. St. L. Broadberry.* Lutterworth.
The Methodist Church: *J. Bates.* REP.
Christianity: *G. Turner.* Edward Arnold.
The Baptists: *J. Wood.* REP.
Who are the Baptists? *W.W. Bottoms.* Baptist Union.
What is a Baptist Church? *L.R. Floyd.* Baptist Union.
Cathedrals: *D. Macauley.* Collins.
Christianity in Action Today: *D.D. Pringle.* Schofield & Sims.
What is the Christian Church? *Schools Council, Journeys into
   Religion.* Granada.
Christian Worship: *J. Rankin.* Lutterworth.
The Orthodox Church: *S. Hackel.* Ward Lock.
The Orthodox Church: *M. Doak.* Wheaton.
Roman Catholicism. *P. Kelly.* Ward Lock.
Visiting a Roman Catholic church: *D. Sullivan.* Lutterworth.

Mosques

The Religious Dimension — Islam: *R. El Droubie and E. Hulmes.*
   Longman.
Islam: *Schools Council, Journeys into Religion.* Granada.
The Religious Dimension — Holy Books: *R. Davies.* Longman.
The Way of the Muslim: *Muhammad Iqbal.* Hulton.

Synagogues

Understanding your Jewish Neighbour: *M. Domnitz.* Lutterworth.
Almonds and Raisins: *M. Mosco.* New English Library.
Scattered Seed: *M. Mosco.* New English Library.
Children's Children: *M. Mosco.* New English Library.

The World of Jewish Faith: *M. Domnitz.* Longman.
Visiting a Synagogue: *D. Charing.* Lutterworth.
A Jewish Family in Britain: *V. Barnett.* RMEP.

Hindu and Sikh Temples
A Hindu Family in Britain: *P. Bridger.* REP.
Thinking About Hinduism: *E.J. Sharpe.* Lutterworth.
Thinking About Sikhism: *W.O. Cole.* Lutterworth.
Visiting a Sikh Temple: *D. Babraa.* Lutterworth.
Sikhism: *W.O. Cole and P. Singh Sambhi.* Ward Lock.
A Sikh Family in Britain: *W.O. Cole.* REP.
The Way of the Sikh: *W.H. McLeod.* Hulton.
Understanding Your Sikh Neighbour: *P. Singh Sambhi.*
    Lutterworth.

Other Meeting Places
The Society of Friends: *G. Gorman.* Wheaton.
The Quakers: *H. Hay.* Ward Lock.
Mormons, Christian Scientists and Jehovah's Witnesses: *L. Beier.*
    Ward Lock.

Christian Festivals
Christmas and its Customs: *G. Hood.* REP.
Stories from the New Testament. *J.R. Bailey.* Beaver Books.
The Christian Faith and its Symbols: *J. Thompson.* Edward Arnold.
Christmas: *A. Ewens.* RMEP.
Festivals and Saints' Days: *V.J. Green.* Blandford.
Shrove Tuesday and Ash Wednesday: *M. Davidson.* RMEP.
Easter: *N. Fairbairn.* RMEP.

Muslim Festivals
A Muslim Family in Britain: *S.W. Harrison and D. Shepherd.* REP.
Ramadan and Id-ul-Fitr: *J. Hannaford.* RMEP.
The Way of the Muslim: *Muhammad Iqbal.* Hulton.

Jewish Festivals
The World of Jewish Faith: *M. Domnitz.* Longman.
Exodus: *L. Uris.* Corgi.
Understanding your Jewish Neighbour: *M. Domnitz.* Lutterworth.
Chanukah: *L. Scholefield.* RMEP.
Passover: *L. Scholefield.* RMEP.
Stories from the Old Testament: *J.R. Bailey.* Beaver Books.
The Jewish World: *D. Charing.* Macdonald.
A Jewish Family in Britain: *V. Barnett.* RMEP.

Hindu Festivals

The Ramayana: *R.K. Narayan*. Viking Press.
Gods, Demons and Others: *R.K. Narayan*. Heinemann.
Divali: *H. Marsh*. RMEP.
A Hindu Family in Britain: *P. Bridger*. REP.
Holi: *J. Hannaford*. RMEP.
Thinking about Hinduism: *E.J. Sharpe*. Lutterworth.
Bhagavad Gita: *J. Mascaro*. Penguin.
Gods and Men: *Bailey, McLeish and Spearman*. OUP.

Sikh Festivals

Understanding your Sikh Neighbour: *P. Singh Sambhi*.
    Lutterworth.
Sikhism: *W.O. Cole and P. Singh Sambhi*. Ward Lock.
The Way of the Sikh: *W.H. McLeod*. Hulton.
Guru Nanak's Birthday: *M. Davidson*. RMEP.

Traditional and Secular Festivals

Stones, Bones and Gods: *R.T. Pearce*. Ward Lock.
English Traditional Customs: *C. Hole*. Batsford.
Chinese Mythology: *A. Christ*. Hamlyn.
Chinese New Year: *A. Bancroft*. RMEP.

General

Church, Synagogue and Temple: *K. Milne*. Wayland.
Five Religions in the Twentieth Century: *W.O. Cole*. Hulton.
Eight Major Religions in Britain: *J. Bradshaw*. Edward Arnold.
Rejoicing in Our Midst: *D.G. Butler*. Edward Arnold.
Festivals and Customs: *N.J. Bull*. Wheaton.
Festivals and Celebrations: *R. Purton*. Blackwell.
Looking at Festivals: *J. Rankin*. Lutterworth.
The Many Faces of Religion: *Dicks, Mennill and Santor*. Ginn.
Calendar of Religious Festivals: *ed. D.F. Brennan*. (Obtainable
    from Shap Working Party, 7 Alderbrook Road, Solihull,
    B91 1NH.)

Further books in this series:

Book Two: Founders, Prophets and Sacred Books.

Book Three: Worship, Ceremonial and Rites of Passage.

Book Four: Religious Leaders and Places of Pilgrimage Today.

Book Five: Religious Beliefs and Moral Codes.

Other books by John Bailey:

Blueprint, Volumes 1 – 4. (Reference books for Secondary School
      Assemblies and R.E.) Pub. Galliard, 1976.

Gods and Men. (Myths and legends from the world's religions.)
      With K. McLeish and D. Spearman. Pub. OUP, 1981.

Themework. (Assembly material for Junior, Middle and Lower
      Secondary Schools.) Pub. Stainer and Bell, 1981.

Stories from the Old Testament. Pub. Beaver Books, 1982.

Stories from the New Testament. Pub. Beaver Books, 1982.